INTROVERT ADVANTAGE

How to Free Yourself From Shyness and Social
Anxiety, Build Confidence and Charisma

(Succeed as an Introvert and Achieve Self Esteem,
and Self Confidence)

James Kress

I0222610

Published by Harry Barnes

James Kress

All Rights Reserved

Introvert advantage: How to Free Yourself From Shyness and Social Anxiety, Build Confidence and Charisma (Succeed as an Introvert and Achieve Self Esteem, and Self Confidence)

ISBN 978-1-7778032-2-3

Legal & Disclaimer

The information contained in this book is not designed to replace or take the place of any form of medicine or professional medical advice. The information in this book has been provided for educational and entertainment purposes only.

The information contained in this book has been compiled from sources deemed reliable, and it is accurate to the best of the Author's knowledge; however, the Author cannot guarantee its accuracy and validity and cannot be held liable for any errors or omissions. Changes are periodically made to this book. You must consult your doctor or get professional medical advice before using any of the suggested remedies, techniques, or information in this book.

Upon using the information contained in this book, you agree to hold harmless the Author from and against any damages, costs, and expenses, including any legal fees potentially resulting from the application of any of the information provided by this guide. This disclaimer applies to any damages or injury caused by the use and application, whether directly or indirectly, of any advice or information presented, whether for breach of contract, tort, negligence, personal injury, criminal intent, or under any other cause of action.

You agree to accept all risks of using the information presented inside this book. You need to consult a professional medical practitioner in order to ensure you are both able and healthy enough to participate in this program.

Table of Contents

Introduction

Nature must have understood the fun in diversity, so it made sure humans' personality is diversified. Human are made in different shades: some are introverted; others are extroverted while the rest of them fall within the line; One day, they seem extroverted and another they appear introverted. More often that not, we are judged by others based on our traits; the characteristics (both physical and behavioural features) we possess as individuals. However, sometimes, an introvert is mistaken for a proud, selfish, snobbish, non-sociable and unfriendly fellow who only cares for nobody but himself. Just because he doesn't associate freely with others; prefers to talk to himself; and does not engage himself with others when having casual conversations he is seen as egotistic and snobbish. On this note of misconception, many people have been wrongly judged especially when you are meeting them for the first time. First impression they say lasts longer. Understanding an individual's personality would, therefore, go a long way in putting an end to the saga of getting mad at someone whom you feel is arrogant when in the real sense, he just wants to have his privacy.

Chapter 1: Understanding Your Introverted Self

It's not surprising that extroverts don't understand introverts, when introverts barely understand themselves.

We already know that we need our space. We already know that we like to think deep. But that's just scratching the surface.

It helps if we know why we like to think deep and why we need our space.

Asking why introverts need small group conversations while extroverts need large group conversations is similar to asking why boys play with cars while girls prefer barbie dolls. In most cases, most boys are proud of playing with their cars while most girls are happy to play with their dolls. The girl who enjoys her dollhouse doesn't care to cross sides and play with cars and action figures. She is happy with what she has.

So why do introverts feel the need to cross over to extroversion?

The answer lies in the fact that we aren't truly fulfilled. We treasure our close friendships, but our close friendships don't always treasure us in return. Our less introverted friends might be interested in small gatherings for a short while, but for the most part, they're going to want to go out into the larger world, and of course, they expect us to come with them without hesitation.

This is where the lack of fulfillment begins to really kick in.

We become too anxious to attend large gatherings, but we feel depressed when we stay home. We process things in our solitude, but it never feels like enough to move us forward.

The whole point of rejuvenation is so that we can be empowered to improve our lives. But the improvement always seems to be short lived instead of long term.

If we had true fulfillment, we wouldn't be experiencing so many of these intensely negative feelings. Our success should be long term, not just a quick bit of indulgence that gets us through the afternoon.

So where is this lack of fulfillment really coming from?

It's coming from a lack of direction in life.

Before we can truly take effective action, we need direction. Whether it's through social conditioning or our own errors, many of us have been mislead into believing that we need to be completely transformed into extroverts. Once introverts come to terms with who they are, they will begin to find direction.

Introverts are no more or less important than extroverts, but everyone plays a unique role. Since you are introverted for a reason, you have a specifically important place in life.

Think of yourself as embarking upon an important mission that only you can fulfill.

When we realize that we are introverted for a reason, we become less likely to fear fate and more likely to embrace destiny.

We are the artists, musicians, writers, readers, intellectuals, and subtle leaders. It's somewhat ironic that many of the things we are good at involve being in the spotlight. The spotlight seems to want us, but we don't want it in return.

We want to become well-known musicians, but we don't want to be up on the stage. We want to be screenplay writers, but we don't want to have to go to interviews or catch too much attention from the media. We want to help others, but we want to stay away from the public eye. We want enough money to live comfortably, but we don't want to attract too much attention through fame.

Instead of dreading the negative side of things, we need to stay focused on the positive side. It's easier to stay focused on the positive side when we know that we're doing the right thing.

If you had ever worked at a dead-end job that you didn't fit into, you probably found it nearly impossible to stay positive when something frustrating happened. This is because you probably subconsciously blamed yourself just for being there in the first place. You knew that even if you got through the negative situation, you would just be right back where you started—empty.

The nagging inner voice doesn't quit.

It's so much easier for children to believe in themselves than adults. Somewhere along the way, we have lost our ability to dream and be realistic at the same time.

Many adults suppress the same inner voice that tries to redirect them to where they're supposed to be. They fear their destiny so much, they feel like they would rather die than pursue it. They tell themselves that it's no big deal to be miserable; it's just a few more decades to go—or maybe seven at the most—and then it will all be over anyway. It seems insane that the main thing that gets them through life is by staying focused on death and anticipating it with great relief.

It doesn't have to be that way.

If you are having difficulty understanding or fully accepting your introverted self, you will need to make some changes in your thinking to gain a new perspective. Making worthwhile changes involves deciding on what we really want, doing what's best, and then feeling secure in our decisions.

Utilizing our inner resources and giving ourselves enough credit to have faith can go a long way. Instead of focusing on everything that can go wrong in the pursuit of our goals, we need to focus on what can go wrong if we don't pursue our goals.

Chapter 2: Overcoming Social Anxiety

As an introvert, your most dreaded situation is most likely attending a social function. Most introverts have social anxiety, which refers to the fear of interacting with others. You may start to fear that those who were invited to the event will negatively judge and evaluate you, causing you to feel inadequate, self-conscious, inferior, depressed and humiliated, even if the day of the event has not arrived yet.

The good news is that it is possible for you to overcome social anxiety. Yes, you are an introvert who dislikes being in a huge crowd, but that does not mean that you won't survive that situation. Overcome your social anxiety with the help of these tips:

Let Go Of All Your Worries

As an introvert, an upcoming social event may cause you to worry intensely. This is the main reason why when you reach the venue, you feel extremely anxious –your constant worrying has actually programmed you to feel anxious even before the event. You can let go of your worries and reverse the trend by visualizing yourself being at the event while displaying your confident and relaxed self.

You can perform this visualization process while sitting in a comfortable chair, taking a warm bath, or meditating. Visualize yourself being at the venue, looking extremely confident and relaxed. Visualize this version of yourself several times over, so that both your mind and body can begin to associate this confident version of yourself with the event. You will notice your worries and anxiety gradually disappear as you perform this visualization activity.

If you can strongly associate this confident version of yourself with the actual event, you will likely surprise yourself by your new found ability to socialize with others without the overwhelming feeling of anxiety. This process is able to take place because you have already programmed your mind and body to work in sync in order to promote confidence.

Confront Your Negative Thoughts

Being an introvert, your social anxiety may cause you to start thinking negative thoughts about yourself once you are in a social situation. You may start to picture yourself looking like a fool in front of a huge crowd of people by performing some humiliating action.

One way to overcome these negative thoughts is to identify them right after they pop into your mind. This will let you determine the exact cause of your social anxiety, thereby allowing you to find ways to deal with it effectively.

Think to yourself "What is the worst that could happen?" if you accidentally say or do something embarrassing. Guess what? No one really cares! Are you going to die just because you said something that may not have been correct? The answer is no. Everyone is so preoccupied with their own lives that they could not care less what you do or say for the most part. It is important to check your ego at the door and allow yourself to make mistakes. Don't let your thoughts bully you around and stop taking yourself so seriously!

Remind yourself that you are competent and strong, and that you are capable of going through whatever social situation you are in...and then just relax. Introverts will often stay holed up in their rooms because they are so afraid of making mistakes in social situations. You simply cannot learn without putting yourself out there and trying things out.

Stop Yourself From Making False, Unrealistic Predictions

Keep in mind that no one can ever predict what will happen in the future. If you allow yourself to make predictions, then you will most likely come up with the worst-case scenarios (scenarios which don't even occur 99.9% of the time); these worst-case scenarios will cause you unnecessary anxiety.

Control what goes on in your mind. Remind yourself that you have full control and power to alter your exaggerated and unrealistic thoughts.

For instance, if you are planning to attend a birthday party, allow your mind to focus on the thought that you will not be the focus of the event. Imagine attending that party while also talking confidently to other guests and enjoying yourself.

No One Is Judging You

You have to keep that fact in mind at all times; it is worth repeating again and again and again. In most cases, social anxiety is the result of over thinking that everyone you encounter will pass judgment on you. It's time to step back, change the way you think about the people around you, and realize the fact that most of them do not focus on you.

In case they really do focus on you, rest assure that their thoughts about you are not as negative as you think. It's time to stop reading people's minds. Remember that you will never know what they are thinking, so why worry about it? Additionally, those around you don't even know the negative, self doubting, and insecure person that you portray in your mind. In actuality, they probably have the same voice in their head and think that you are the one judging them.

TAKE ACTION! Start attending social functions, so that you can practice altering your negative thoughts about yourself. It can be hard to get yourself out there as an introvert, but it is well worth it!

Embrace Your Nerves

Are you feeling a little nervous, scared or uncomfortable when thinking about yourself at an upcoming social event? Attend the event anyway. Despite your social anxiety and discomfort, it is still beneficial to got to the venue instead of not attending. You can always leave early, but try to push yourself to stay as long as you can. When you get home, write down how the experience went in a journal so you can keep track of how your anxiety levels change from event to event.

Slowly stretch your boundaries. You can do this by desensitizing yourself from one uncomfortable and awkward situation at a time. Just like any learned skill, your ability to master socializing takes time and practice.

You will notice that you get better and better each time you attend a social function. You will also realize that despite your nerves, deciding to stretch your boundaries in a gradual manner can help you grow and develop your ability to be involved in witty banters with the people around you. Eventually, you can master

15

the art of opening and maintaining healthy conversations when you are in social settings.

Drop The Introvert Label

This does not mean that you should be ashamed of your personality, or that you should pretend to be outgoing or extroverted when you are not. It just means that you have to stop restricting your personality simply because you are termed an introvert. Being a natural introvert does not mean that you can't talk.

If you continue to put a label on your personality, then you will find it hard to improve yourself and make the necessary adjustments in order to become more social. It does not hurt to have a few acquaintances, or to initiate small talk and conversation once in a while.

Instead of continuing to label your personality, remind yourself that all people are in the same boat, aiming to share the same special and unique human connections with the people they meet.

Develop An Exposure Hierarchy

Exposure hierarchy refers to a list containing certain situations that trigger your anxiety. The written entries on the list are arranged based on the level of severity. To make use of the exposure hierarchy, you need to start by performing the easiest, least frightening behavior on the list, and continue to move onto more fearful tasks until you reach the task that embodies the pinnacle of your fear.

To make an exposure hierarchy, write down ten situations that cause you to be anxious, especially when in a social setting. Rate each one – with zero indicating that you don't feel anxious and 100 indicating the most severe case of anxiety for you.

This will assist you in determining what exactly triggers you to be anxious when attending a social event. You can then expose yourself to your triggers gradually until you no longer feel controlled by anxiety when you are facing them.

You are capable of developing your ability to socialize even if you are an introvert. By just following a few simple tips, you can improve your communication skills while lowering your social anxiety, which will lead you to more opportunities for success in both your professional and personal relationships.

Chapter 3: Introverts Personality Traits

Who is an introvert?

Introvert comes from Latin intro-, "inward," and vertere, "turning." It describes a person who tends to turn inward mentally. Introverts sometimes avoid large groups of people, feeling more energized by time alone. The opposite of an introvert is an extrovert; who finds energy in interactions with others.

Signs You're Really an Introvert

It can be difficult to admit to yourself that you may be an introvert. When we think of people as being introverted, we often wrongly assume that they are people who don't like people. However, as Susan Cain so effectively showed the world in her book, Quiet: The Power of Introverts in a World That Can't Stop talking, introverts can be warm, interested in others, and powerful in their own right. Yet the stigma many still attach to being an introvert may lead people otherwise inclined to have these tendencies to resist if not deny them within themselves.

These nine behavioral signs of introversion can give you a start in learning about traits and attitudes that suggest your own personality may be less outer-oriented than you realize. See how many you feel honestly apply to you:

You enjoy having time to yourself. When you have the chance to take a break, you'd rather spend time reading, playing video games, or just listening to music. That quiet time is important to your sense of well-being even though there are plenty of times that you enjoy social get-togethers.

Your best thinking occurs when you're by yourself. You're not opposed to group meetings or discussions, but if you want to come up with a creative solution, you need some time to work the problem out on your own. Having the opportunity to reflect quietly on a problem allows you to make the maximum use of your ability to engage in original thought, and to produce results about which you can feel proud.

You lead best when others are self-starters. Despite the belief that introverts are so quiet that they can't step up to the plate and run things, under the right circumstances they can be the best leaders of all. If the group is ready to lead itself, then the introverted leader will draw the most potential out of them. It's only when the group needs a spark provided by its head that introverts might be unable to provide the necessary guidance. Then you'll need to partner with an extroverted yin to your yang.

You're the last to raise your hand when someone asks for something from a group. As you might remember from your elementary school days, there were some fellow students whose hands shot straight up into the air when the teacher asked a question or needed someone to volunteer. Extraverts tend to be ready and eager to stand out in any academic or social situation. You are probably more of an introvert than an extravert if you are content to sit back and let others take center stage. It's not that introverts know less than others; they just don't feel a particular need to be in that limelight.

Other people ask you your opinion. Just as introverts are less likely to volunteer in public situations, they are also less likely to volunteer opinions or advice in less public settings. Whether it's a family discussion around the kitchen table or a staff meeting to decide how to market new products, people high in introversion will keep their views to themselves and let the noisy extraverts take control. Because of this, and because your advice may indeed be highly valued, it's likely that if you're constantly being asked "What do you think?" it might suggest that your behavior sends cues to others of your inner desire to focus your attention and thoughts inward.

You often wear headphones when you're in a public situation. Whether it's making your way through a crowded bus station or just navigating a crowded street, if you're an introvert you most likely don't seek a great deal of contact with others. In decades past, if you wanted to avoid interacting with strangers, you would keep your head down and look straight in front of you. Now you have the added protection of being able to hide behind the protection of your headphones (though no one has to know whether there's actually music coming through them or not).

You prefer not to engage with people who seem angry or upset. You're likely to try to avoid people who seem like they might be in a bad mood, if not outright furious at something or someone. According to research by University College London psychologist Marta Ponari and collaborators, people high in introversion fail to show what's called the "gaze-cuing effect." Normally, if you were to see the image of a person's face on a computer screen looking in a certain direction, you would follow that person's gaze and therefore respond more quickly to a visual target on that side of the screen than when the person's gaze and the target are pointed in opposite directions. Introverts show this effect just as extraverts do, but if the person's face seems angry, they don't show the gaze-cuing effect.

This suggests that people high in introversion don't want to look at someone who seems mad. Ponari and her team believe that this is because they are more sensitive to potentially negative evaluations. If you think a person is angry because of something to do with you, his or her gaze becomes a threat.

You receive more calls, texts, and emails than you make, unless you have no choice. All other things being equal, people high in introversion don't reach out voluntarily to their social circles. If they have a few minutes to spare, they won't initiate a call just to pass the time by socializing. Similarly, they don't generate emails and other written correspondence but instead react to the communications they receive from others. It's quite likely that if you're a true introvert you would avoid jobs in which you have to engage in such outreach, such as becoming a telemarketing representative. If you have no choice but to initiate communications, such as when you invite people to a social event, you will be less likely to pick up the phone and make a call and more likely to send your request through cyberspace or the post office. This may relate to the desire not to be evaluated. By calling people, you risk being told "no" in person, which you may find demoralizing. When the request happens asynchronously (that is, not in real time), you may get the same turn-down but in a way that may allow you to save face, if not self-esteem.

You don't initiate small talk with salespeople or others with whom you have casual contact. It's nearly impossible for you to imagine yourself being like that the garrulous individual in front of you in line at the supermarket who chats with everyone about the weather. If you're late or stressed, you don't "leak" this information out to the people around you but instead just think it quietly to yourself as you mull over your plight. You may feel that it's no one's business but your own, or you may prefer to come out of your bad mood through your own personal stress-busting strategies. Either way, people don't really know how you're feeling or thinking at any given moment, unless you feel close enough to them to share these private reflections.

Being an introvert definitely has its advantages. You're less likely to make a social gaffe, such as by inadvertently insulting someone whose opinion you don't agree with. Because you enjoy reflecting on your own thoughts, you'll be less likely to get bored when you're alone than someone who needs constant social stimulation. The only risk you face is that people who don't know you might think you're aloof or that you feel superior to everyone else. Giving yourself permission to be a little more open in revealing your thoughts and feelings may help you make the best of both worlds, being true to your personality while not erring in the direction of seeming antisocial.

If, on the other hand, you're an all-out extravert, you might benefit from practicing a little introversion in your daily life. See what it's like not to be the first one to speak, take charge, or offer your opinion. It's possible that allowing yourself to tap into your secret introvert may help you experience the world in a new, more reflective manner.

Chapter 4: Waking Up From A Dream

According to Don Miguel Ruiz, we've been living in a dream. In his masterpiece The Four Agreements, Don Miguel Ruiz shares his powerful insight on how society works. We are born in complete innocence and limitless potential. As we grow, we are introduced to the "dream of the planet". Everyone can dream, and everyone's dream is different. We are all experiencing different realities. Together, however, we make up the "dream of the planet", which is composed of rules and standards we must follow. We are spoon fed this dream through rewards and punishment and few of us ever question it. The result? We get a human being wasting away their entire life through actions dictated by the validation of others. We get a human being reduced to the likes of a dog that acts only to receive approval of its master, behaves well so it may be rewarded, and avoids any wrong for fear of punishment. The worst part is that the dog never once questions the status quo.

Being an introvert in an extroverted society means not fitting into their 'dream' of how a human being should be or behave. However, this is just the tip of the iceberg. The scenario painted by Don Miguel Ruiz can leave you contemplating about even deeper existential problems.

Understanding this allows you to make sense out of why people act the way they do. It explains why there may have been those that put you down in the past. Perhaps, like me, you weren't accepted. However, whatever was done to you came from a place of unconscious action. Those around you bought into the idea that people should behave in a specific way and attacked those who didn't fit the bill. Chances are, they themselves didn't fit it and projected their insecurities onto you. If this occurred to you, I ask that you don't judge them or hold any resentment. They were acting based on the ideas and paradigms they held. People can only give out what they have inside.

Growing up people around me put me down constantly. "You're ugly. You're disgusting." Bullies made fun of me on a daily basis as I walked from class to class. I would receive a shove from time to time, and I simply accepted it. I was too scared to fight back. My self-image deteriorated and my self-confidence banished. The constant ridicule provided fertile ground for limiting beliefs to grow. I thought the problem was me. "I'm ugly." "I'm short." "I'm fat." "Girls won't like me." I was buying to their reality. And guess what? I blamed it on my introversion. "If only I was an extrovert like them, then I'd be cool too", I thought.

I turned to books in search of answers to my problems. The more I read, the more I realized how mistaken I was for believing these things to be true. The only one to blame for the anxiety and limiting beliefs I held was me, for accepting them into my psyche in the first place. These limiting beliefs were not inherently mine; I had 'picked them up' from others. I thought, "Then, who am I?" I began playing with thought experiments. "If I were to separate my sense of 'self' from these negative labels, what would I be left with?"

This marked the beginning of a beautiful journey called introspection. I turned within. I identified myself, my desires, and my essence. I discovered who I really was and what I could be capable of. It wasn't overnight; it was more of an ever-evolving process. I stopped taking things personally. At a core level, my sense of identity had become unshakeable. I was grounded in me. The point of reference for my actions became my feelings and intuition, not what others expected of me. All of this happened as a result of asking myself the following questions:

What do I really want?

Do I really want to do what I'm doing?

Am I doing it for me, or for somebody else?

Am I acting from a sense of trying to please others or am I acting from a sense of freedom?

Do I really want to be an extrovert? Or am I not happy just being me and would rather be accepted for who I was?

Do this if you haven't already. Begin a journey of introspection. You're an introvert. I honestly believe introverts have the greatest power for turning inward to change their outward reality. What are humans if not the creators of their experience?

Chapter 5: The Workplace

Surprise: your job has a tremendous impact on your life.[68] On average, we spend 20% of our waking lives in the workplace, and that number rises to approximately 24% of our entire lives (including sleep time) during a typical 50-year employment period.[69] If that statistic doesn't depress you, then this one will: according to a 2017 survey conducted by the Faas Foundation, 71% of people reported they are unhappy with their current jobs.[70] Taken together, those stats tell us that most of us are unhappy for at least a quarter of our lives.

But all hope is not lost. Although the question of whether you should be looking for a different or better way to earn a living is ultimately outside the scope of this book, by the end of this chapter, you will have multiple tactics and strategies for improving your relationships in the workplace.

The Proper Environment: CLIF Careers

Most of us work in a traditional office with at least a few other people working in it five days a week. Even if you are a solo entrepreneur working from your home office, you have suppliers, customers, and vendors, and that means you will need to apply interpersonal communication skills to build effective commercial relationships. If you have found the holy grail of economic prosperity that allows you to sit back and make money without talking to anyone, then congratulations. You've finished the book and don't need to read any further. Also, give me your phone number and email address because you're my new hero. For the rest of us, let's focus on making where we spend the majority of our time more tolerable.

For the rest of us, we need to go find a C.L.I.F. And in case anyone gets any ideas about suing me, I did not mean go kill yourself. I can't believe I actually had to say that. Anyhow, back to this C.L.I.F.

concept. As stated and restated throughout the course of this book, when society rigs the game in favor of extraverts, be proactive about rigging it in the opposite direction. This advice is no less important when applied to the workplace. We can't have better, more meaningful relationships at work if our job environment doesn't align with our personality. When it comes to introverts in the workplace, we have more success and better relationships when our jobs entail the following elements:[71]

C = Creativity

L = Low Maintenance

I = Independence

F = Focus

Creativity

Some of the greatest artists and writers in history have been successful in their craft because they have the power to imagine, visualize a masterpiece, and ultimately execute that vision into a practical and commercially viable deliverable.[72] The most successful introverted writers in history, including Joan Didion, Susan Cain, J.K. Rowling, and Dr. Seuss, all channeled their creativity to produce commercial works of literature that the world loved and were willing to pay money to read.[73] Likewise, artists such as Jimi Hendrix, Elvis Presley, Steven Spielberg, and Gustave Moreau used similar methods to produce immortal songs, movies, paintings, sculptures, and other forms of art that were wildly successful from a commercial perspective. [74]

Low Maintenance

As discussed above, as introverts, we are traditionally low-maintenance individuals.[75] We don't mind being alone, and we're better at conserving energy than wasting it. We dislike micromanagement and often prefer being left to our own devices. The benefit to our managers in the workplace – especially those that are too busy to teach their direct reports – is that we're resourceful and don't need constant oversight. Jobs with managers that want to supervise your activities down to the most ministerial of tasks are not going to be a good fit for you or any other introvert on this planet.

Independence

Along a similar vein, because we're so low-maintenance, we often can, and prefer to, work independently. Managers and clients that can offer us latitude to provide our own direction on a particular job or project will likely work well with us.

The Best CLIF Careers for Introverts

Below, and in no particular order, are some examples of CLIF careers based on the work environment that they traditionally provide. Wage information was obtained from estimates for 2018 published by the United States Department of Labor Bureau of Labor Statistics (the "BLS").[76] If you live outside the United States, you'll want to check publications from the comparable regulatory authority for more accurate median pay figures.

Artist

According to the BLS, there are two types of artists: craft artists, who create functional art, and fine artists, such as painters and sculptors, who create art that is purely aesthetic. Both offer work settings that are suited for an introverted personality. Not only are you able to express your creativity in a ceramic, textile, or illustrative setting, for the most part, you are also working independently. Your work environment is typically a studio space or, often times, your own home. 2018 U.S. median pay: $40,490 for craft artists and $58,370 for fine artists.

Graphic Designer

Graphic design is another profession that necessarily requires creativity and working independently. Often, individuals in this profession choose to be self-employed. Even those that are not are pleased to find that, similar to artists, their work products and skill sets are so unique and subjective that they don't naturally lend themselves to micromanagement, which results in a low-maintenance work environment. Given the isolated nature of the work, it requires a considerable amount of focus and private working time. 2018 U.S. median pay: $54,680.

Similar professions that involve the use of creativity include photographers (2018 U.S. median pay: $42,770), who often freelance and have broad discretion on the photos taken and selected for publication, and film and video editors (2018 U.S. median pay: $86,830), which was one of the higher-paying creative jobs in 2018 and similarly entails copious amounts of quiet, private time, and focus.

Software Engineer

Of the traditional career paths for introverts, software engineer is generally one of the more lucrative ones. Software engineers use computer programming languages to build, test, and improve how efficient and effective software programs are.[77] Software engineers may specialize in any number of areas, including networks, operating systems, applications, or databases.[78] This role generally involves a substantial amount of independent work and focus. 2018 median pay: $103,438.

IT Manager

If you have a computer science and technology skill set, but don't want to pursue a career in software engineering, you may want to consider the role of IT manager. These positions generally allow you to manage the security and operation of an organization's information systems. You would be responsible for handling software and hardware upgrades, managing a technology budget, and fulfilling or delegating the fulfillment of "helpdesk" tickets. In this "low maintenance" role, you would be responsible for managing the work of others, but as the overseer of an entire discipline within a company, this position would afford you independence and the ability to utilize your natural leadership talents. 2018 median pay: $83,896.

Forensic Scientist

If you, like many introverts, thrive in detail-oriented tasks, you may also want to consider a career as a forensic scientist. Like any other scientist, a forensic scientist is responsible for collecting and analyzing evidence, which requires a delicate eye and careful treatment of minutiae. Unlike other scientists, the forensic scientist's work is ultimately applied in the legal system, which, for criminal matters, means that the scientific analyses and tests conducted by the forensic scientist could play an instrumental role in exonerating or convicting an accused person. The hours of detail-oriented testing and analysis in this extremely rewarding profession generally suits an introverted personality. 2018 median pay: $62,490.

Accounting Manager

If math is your forte, consider a position as an accounting manager. In this role, you would oversee and manage the day-to-day operations of an accounting department, including analyzing data, creating financial reports, and developing organizational accounting policies.[79] As in the case of an IT manager, you will be responsible for some oversight and management of others, but you will also have greater independence and control over your craft and your work environment. 2018 median pay: $78,638.

Auto Mechanic

Finally, if you're handy and enjoy cars, but not all of the attention that they come with, being an auto mechanic may be a good fit for you. As a mechanic, you would be responsible for inspecting, repairing, and performing maintenance on motor vehicles, using a variety of tools and technologies to perform your job, and you would have the flexibility to specialize in specific systems or vehicle types.[80] Although you likely wouldn't enjoy peace and quiet, you could spend large blocks of time doing focused work in an independent work setting. 2018 median pay: $38,979.

Introverts and The Job Interview

If you're an introvert who's currently between jobs, you're probably fearing destitute unemployment far less than the inevitable series of job interviews that finding a job entails. This is to be expected, especially considering that the job interview "culture" is a deck that is largely stacked against the introvert. According to executive search recruiter and award-winning author Barry Deutsch, most job interviews are designed for an extravert to thrive.[81] It is an open discussion with strangers where you are asked to talk about yourself, reveal information, and come up with quick, and often trite or "slick," responses to scenario-based questions that often do not end up sounding genuine.

Another reason why we struggle during the interview process is because we, as introverts, generally do not make good first impressions.[82] Most of us are reserved and cautious during first encounters, and we usually require more exposure to a new person before warming up to them. Our tendency to be reserved during a first meeting with someone is usually misconstrued, often incorrectly or unfairly, as evidence that we are shy or anti-social, or that we lack interpersonal skills. Unfortunately, in a job interview setting, an adverse first impression means that you won't get a chance to make a second one.

In addition, introverts process information carefully and think before they speak. Unfortunately, this trait is also misinterpreted as unpreparedness, as a hiring manager expects an immediate response. This, too, is designed to favor the extravert, as introverts would prefer to hear a question and then let their creative tendencies go to work to come up with the perfect answer. The common result of these misconceptions and systemic disadvantages for introverts is that we are often relegated to the role of contingency candidate, if not outright rejected, during the interview process, and the result is a lost economic opportunity.[83]

Naturally, hiring managers would prefer a canned, Pavlovian answer to a more thoughtful and genuine one. Or perhaps they want to indulge in the illusion that a genuine and deliberate answer can be formulated on the fly in a manner of nanoseconds. In any case, effectively, your charge is to prove to the interviewer that: (i) you can anticipate the interviewer's question, despite the irony that such an event necessarily reflects poorly on the interviewer's ability to thoughtfully craft such questions; and (ii) you can answer the question in a way that comes across as simultaneously candid and sporadic. Yeah. I know.

Flipping the tables can be done, uncomfortable though it may be, through preparation:

Research. Research the company and the interviewers, and commit to memory the key bullets in the job posting (if available). Read the company's annual report (if public) or "About Us" and related pages on the company's website. If you were the interviewer, based on what you know about the company and the decision-makers, what three things would you want to know about a candidate? What unique skills, perspectives, experiences, or other advantages do you have that someone else won't? Write down the questions, then answer them in written form. Prepare a list of questions for the interviewer. You'll need to use them anyway at the end of the interview.

Practice. Practice reading your responses to those questions out loud in front of the mirror. What key words/phrases do you need to memorize to create the illusion of authenticity? If you don't live alone, ask your spouse, roommate, or partner to block out 10 minutes from their oh-so-busy schedules (but don't use that tone when you ask them) to help you out. Trust me. They're going to find out anyway when they overhear you practicing in front of the mirror, and it's worth the temporary awkwardness to get some real-time rehearsal. Practice until you feel comfortable with a few small talking points that you can rely on in a pinch. Practice segue phrases. For example: "ya know, for me, it all comes back to [experience/education/other advantage]…"

Divert and Deflect. If, during the interview process, you get stumped, use the list of interviewer questions and your segue phrases to bail yourself out. Counter-questions like "Can you tell me what you mean by…" or "Can you give me an example of…" can accomplish any one or more of the following goals: (1) shifts the discomfort back to the interviewer; (2) gives you more time to think about the question; and (3) forces the interviewer to rephrase the question, which often gives you clues as to the million dollar answer they're wanting to hear.

Using the above strategies before and during the interview will keep the interview flowing smoothly, capsize the ship of extravert-friendly bias, and ultimately, increase your chances of getting interview #2.

Tailoring Your Current Job to Your Personality

The careers listed above suit an introvert's personality and skill set, but your career field may not have any of these options. Identifying your strengths and weaknesses and comparing them to your daily responsibilities is a way to determine if you have the ability to stand out or if talking to your boss about adjusting your responsibilities to better suit your personality is the next step. So what do you do if your current work environment mixes with your introversion like a straw hat in a tornado, but you're not in a position to switch jobs?

Here are a few suggestions for thriving at your current place of work:

1. Try to find a quiet space. If you are in an office with too many distractions, try to find a spot farther from the noise, or a place like a conference room where you can close the door (see below).

2. Use communication tools that play to your strengths. Thinking on your feet and reacting quickly are required when you make phone calls or have face-to-face meetings. Conversely, e-mail is perfect for a slower, more well-thought-out message.

3. Lobby for a work-from-home arrangement. If it is impossible to work as well in your office, suggest to your supervisor an arrangement where you can work from home 1-2 days per week.

Technology has come a long way in allowing workers to stay connected, even from home. Before discussing with your boss, figure out how you can track and measure your productivity, then compare the results from your work-from-home days with your office days. If the results show that you're more productive at home versus in the office, discuss the results with your boss and use them to support your case for a work-from-home arrangement.

Your Quiet Place: The Conference Room Dealing with Collaboration

For those situations where collaboration is required, Monster[84] career expert, author, and consultant Vicki Salemi also offers advice on how to deal with others during live, in-person meetings. According to Salemi, your strength in in-person meetings lies in your listening, not your spoken word.[85] Most introverts, she posits, are more adept at listening, taking notes, and engaging in mental problem-solving. Using this time to process information and perform an introspective analysis allows us to revert to stakeholders at a later time with a fully-conceived solution to the identified problem.

A second technique for survival during live in-person meetings lies in preparation. Introverts who outline their ideas and key talking points are less likely to perish under the stage fright of a live meeting. It also will allow you to get that word in edgewise, as it's far easier to speak readily, even with the local loudmouths, if you have your thoughts prepared and in front of you.

One issue that introverts have working in the group setting is the perceived inefficiency. Often times, introverts in a group project setting believe that they could accomplish the stated objective quicker and more effectively if they were able to work alone. And sometimes, or maybe a lot of the time, it's…true? To be fair, though, given favorable assumptions, having a few extra helping hands in these situations can actually be beneficial. The solution? Leadership.

When it comes to a collaborative job or project, you should volunteer for the leadership role at your first given opportunity.[86] While it may seem counterintuitive, being assertive in this limited scenario will actually make you less uncomfortable for the rest of the project.

As discussed above, as an introvert, leadership is in your DNA. You will be far more capable of tolerating, if not enjoying, whatever project you're working on if you have some level of control over the outcome.

Dealing with Specific Types of Extraverts: The Filibusterer, The Prairie Dog, and The HIPAA-Potamus

We are introverts. There are people who will make us uncomfortable, nervous, or overstimulated. And then there are people who conjure within us a hatred that would scorch a thousand suns. To call them annoying would be an insult to Fran Drescher, Steve Urkel, Kimmy Gibbler, and Screech Powers. In a workplace environment, these minions of extraversion not only conflict with our personality and thwart our productivity, but they threaten our very existence. And the worst part? Because of our inherent low-maintenance demeanor and aversion to rocking the boat or creating awkwardness, we can't – or at least won't - do a damn thing about it.

OK, fine. It's not that bad, but still. They're more irritating than a pair of wool undies. Without further ado, allow me to introduce the triumvirate of banality: (1) the filibusterer; (2) the prairie dog; and (3) the HIPAA-Potamus.

The Filibusterer

The filibusterer is notorious for popping her head into your office for "just a second" or stopping you in the hallway for a "quick question," and it's only after 15 minutes of non-stop, mindless banter that you realized you've been sucked into another dimension of verbal Peruvian torture. To exacerbate matters, the filibusterer seems to somehow have read your calendar, as they always manage to stop by less than five minutes before a conference call, meeting, or other scheduled appointment because, of course, whatever sort of gossip they've been dying to unload on someone simply cannot wait. If it's not Greg's breath, Colleen's hideous nails, or Merle's failure to follow the proper channels when setting up a purchase order, it's some other piece of trivial news or opinion that you wouldn't be interested in even if such knowledge could somehow decrypt the meaning of your life. In short, they're not evil people, but let me put it this way: if your mental state was a knife, they would somehow grind it into a spoon.

If, like me, you want them to leave faster than they appeared, but don't want to hurt anyone's feelings (let's face it:

filibusterers aren't jerks, they're just annoying), here are a few tips for building a graceful parachute:

Mention the time and feign surprise. Letting people know that the time is stressing you out will signal that they shouldn't take any more of it from you. "Oh wow, it's already 11:30. Where did my morning go?" or something similar usually does the trick.

Refer to your next meeting and suggest an alternate time. If you notice that it's close to a half-hour milestone – when most meetings are scheduled – mention that you're preparing for that meeting when they come in, then suggest catching up at an alternate time. "Hey, I'm about to hop into a 3:30, but can we catch up at 4?" will get them to clear out while preserving the goodwill between you two.

Get up and leave. Not without explanation, of course, but try something like "Heading to go see [XYZ colleague], you walking that way?" This forces them to decide whether or not to follow you around. Unless they have separation issues or happen to have to see the same person at the same time, they shouldn't.

Fill your chairs. The easiest way to make people to leave is to make them uncomfortable while they're visiting. If you have an office or a sitting area in your cubicle, fill the chairs with files, books, or anything that would create an obstacle to sitting down. It's a subtle way of saying "Sorry, I'd love for you to have a comfortable place to talk for the duration of this visit, but the chairs have no room for your butt."

The Prairie Dog

If you work in an open workspace or cubicle station, you've probably been exposed to the prairie dog. This type of extravert is so filled with solutions she just can't help but eavesdrop on your conversations and offer you unsolicited advice at every opportunity. She also is unaware that your cubicle boundaries contain invisible walls that extend up to the ceiling.

Dealing with prairie dogs are a bit trickier because the annoyance factor arises not from the amount of time taken away, but from the immediate and surprising nature of the distraction. It goes without saying that the most effective approach would be to have a candid, but polite and respectful talk with the offender and offer one or more of the several hundred reasons why prairie dogging is not polite or appropriate. If that's not your thing, however, here are a few less confrontational ways to get your message across:

Go for the Oscar. A little drama never hurt anyone. The next time you get prairie dogged, act as though you've been startled from an 8-hour sleep. A little jump and some theatrics followed by a matter-of-fact "you scared the crap outta me!" could be a subtle reminder that a prairie dog introduction is unsettling.

Build a Bigger Wall. Filed under the more elaborate passive-aggressive strategies for keeping prairie dogs off your property is to decorate the top boundaries of your cubicle with seasonal or similar accessories that eliminate the hand grips necessary for prairie doggery. Check your employee handbook for guidelines of what types of decoration are appropriate. I'm guessing what's permitted lies somewhere between deadly metal spikes and some tasteful border art. If you can't find something that works, then petition your manager for a larger file cabinet or other work-related appliance that obstructs the view from your neighbor.

Out of Sight, Out of Sound. Prairie dogging is popular because people are lazy, and popping your head above a relatively short partition wall takes less time than having to walk around to the other person's cubicle entrance. Wearing headphones and positioning your reading or working space facing away from the border between you and the prairie dog effectively eliminates that perceived efficiency.

The HIPAA-Potamus

The Health Insurance Portability and Accountability Act of 1996 ("HIPAA") was signed into law in order to provide Americans with a modicum of privacy when it came to their health issues. The HIPAA-Potamus takes those privacy rights, stomps on them a few hundred times, chews on them for a few minutes, and then spits them out into your face with the velocity of 60 hurricanes. I'm talking about that co-worker that confuses the name on your door with a Medical Degree or Doctorate of Psychology Degree.

The HIPAA-Potamus takes advantage of your politeness and treats it as an open invitation to share with you far too much information about their medical issues, social or personal life, or other non-work-related shit that you don't have the time or patience to deal with. Your attitude is probably not as unforgiving as the foregoing sentence, and like the Filibusterer, the HIPAA-Potamus is not a malicious counterpart (jury's still out on the Prairie Dog). Furthermore, although they can occasionally be self-involved to a mildly annoying degree, you can almost certainly sympathize with the HIPAA-Potamus and her plight, and you don't want to piss off karma by slapping away a well-intentioned hand that only asks for someone to listen and perhaps offer some helping words. The good news is that there is a single solution that is both polite and appropriate: the handoff. Referring them to a doctor, psychologist, another qualified professional, or even someone in the Human Resources Department (preferably the one with the patronizing voice that couldn't sound genuine if her life depended on it) is the most effective way to solve their problem. It will also free up 10-20 minutes per day that you would otherwise never get back.

Chapter 6: The Good Sides Of Being An Introvert

I wrote this chapter not to make you happy about your good side or to make you sad about your bad side. I just want to point you how you can develop and improve.

4.1 Signs that reveal whether you are introverted

While the stereotypical point of view is that introverts are very easy to recognize, for example, they are those who at the parties will always stand by and fiddle with their phone. However, someone who interacts well in a group can also be an introvert. People often do not realize that they are introverts because they think introversion is about being shy but there are many signs that would indicate whether we are introverts. Check out some of them.

1. You struggle with small talk

I already said something about this subject, but I think introverted people should give a small talk a chance. It just means you should give people a chance by talking with them if they feel the need to tell you something.

2. You are going to parties, but not to meet people

If you are introverted, sometimes you may want to go to a social event but never do, or you go but do not meet new people. Most introverts at parties spend time with people they already know. If you happen to meet a new person, that's fine, but that was never your intention.

3. You often feel lonely in a crowd

If you feel like an outsider at social gatherings even if there are people you know present, you're probably an introverted type. Okay, I must say I still feel lost when I am in a crowd, and I just do not like it.

4. Networking causes hives

What is normal for some people, which is networking in order to achieve better business contacts," you feel fake.

5. Sometimes people tell you that you're "too intense"

If you are prone to deep philosophical discussions and cultivate a love for literature and films that are an intellectual challenge, most likely you're an introvert.

6. You can easily be distracted

While extroverts are bored when they are not surrounded by enough variety, introverts have the opposite problem: they often feel burdened in environments where the stimulation comes from different sources.

7. You think of a vacation as productive time

8. To speak before 500 people is less stressful to you than you to talk to them in person later

9. In public transport, you prefer to sit on the edge of chairs, not in the middle

10. If you are very active, you start to lose energy fast

11. You would rather be an expert in one area but spread on more areas

12. You have a constant inner monologue

13. People have been calling you "old soul" since your 20s

14. People often tell you to get "out of your shell."

So, introversion represents a person's orientation toward his inner world in which he seeks stimulation and content that is emotionally satisfying and enriching. Introverted people are perceived as loners and those who do not like large groups of people and do not like to stay long within. Unlike them, extroverted people seek stimulation in the outside world, they are social, and it's easy for them to get in contact with new people.

According to scientists and psychiatrists introverts obtained theirs energy from individual activities, such as reading, fishing, walking, while extroverted prefer socializing and interacting with others. While the extroverts enjoy large and crowded places, the introverted person will tell you that it is psychologically tiring. The fact is that some of the most important historical figures were introverts. I will list just a few: Gandhi, Edison, Leonardo da Vinci, Alfred Hitchcock, Albert Einstein ... Albert Einstein was even in the first years of schooling considered mentally retarded because he did not fit in the German schooling system which is largely based on extroversion. Until he moved to Italy, the young Albert had rotten grades, and he was even recommended to repeat the classes. Arriving in Italy, he met with a much different system of education that allowed individualism, and there's where Albert began to show the first signs of his genius. Painters, poets, and writers are largely introverted.

Writers in many cases transfer their introversion to their characters such are Sherlock Holmes, character of withdrawn mathematician from the movie "A Beautiful Mind" and Spielberg's Captain John Miller from the film "Saving Private Ryan" played by Tom Hanks. After all, how often do you hear that a writer loves crazy parties?

The big problem introverted people have is that today's culture is based on extroversion. Openness, expressed sociality and activity are considered good qualities. Today's society forces teamwork, which the introvert cannot handle because he achieves best results individually. People do not realize that introversion is a human trait, not a disease or disorder of any kind. Therefore, it is important to point it out to them because it will lead to easier understanding of introverted persons.

The assumption is that about 25% of the populations are introverts. Also, the problem occurs because teachers in schools are not familiar with this topic, and are unable to establish whether the child is introverted, or if a problem is something else. Children are placed under the category of "shy" and there ends any work with them. Introverted people, still have enormous potential because they can focus longer on a specific problem and to solve it much better than extroverted. While extroverted people give little importance to some things, introverts like to analyze deeply and to give it attention. Introverted people, in many cases have the ability to perceive the tiniest details.

"It's not that I'm so smart, it's just that I stay with problems longer." Albert Einstein For introverted people is believed that they do not like to talk much, but that is not the true. They just do not like to talk if they do not have anything clever to say. I do not like to chat, but prefer topics that require deep thinking so I resent small talks that take away my precious energy.

Ask me something that interests me and I can talk for hours. Also, introverts do not engage in conversation if they are not fully familiar with the matter. In this case, they only listen and absorb. Also, because they are not shy, introversion has nothing to do with modesty and these people have no fear of people, but simply do not like to be engaged in talks with everyone.

In the end, introverts are responsible for some of the greatest inventions in mankind because if were not for their introversion, the world would look completely different. Here is another official data that will help introverted people to more easily accept their connection to society and to be more secure in their abilities. The introversion increases with high IQ. Among the highly gifted people, there is a total of 75% of introverted people.

Introverted people just prefer to be alone, to spend time in solitude to preserve energy while time spent with other people can be very tiring and exhausting for them. They are preoccupied with the internal world: the world of thoughts, dreams, pictures and words. The need of an introverted person to be alone is not a sign of depression, but something that is necessary for them in order to regain their balance. I am a typical example of an introvert: I love silence, solitude, avoid crowds, meetings and everything that involves a large number of people. Although I'm introspective, I like to have long conversations while I do not like trivial stories and a waste of time (the phone is my biggest "enemy").

1.Introverts are very creative and a little (or a lot) eccentric. Some consider them to be strange, but I would like to call them (us) individualists.

2.Although they seem shy, they are brave enough to do public work, to help others and to share their thoughts and ideas with people.

3.They avoid conflicts, but when they speak out about something, you can be sure they stand firmly on their point of view.

4.They are not interested in superficial things.

5.Introverts like to talk, they just do not like banal chit-chat, and they prefer long, meaningful conversations.

6.Introverts are honest, and you can always have confidence in the honesty of their emotions.

7.Introverts are patient. Thanks to their ability to have fun even in solitude and to get lost in their thoughts, it is easier for them to wait.

8.They never make important decisions in a hurry. They think about everything in details and are rarely impulsive.

10.Introverts do not like negative and emotionally draining people. Yes, they can be good friends and someone who "knows how to listen," but if you abuse their honesty, you will find they stop answering your calls.

11.When an introvert expresses his opinion or finally speaks about what bothered him for long, it shocks other people because of their belief that it is a shy person who cannot utter a bad word. Introverts sometimes keep their thinking to themselves for a long time, so they would not have to enter into conflict or hurt another person. When this happens, they do not look back.

12.Introverts can't become extroverts. If you want to get to know an introverted person, you should have a lot of patience. I have been told it took five years to get to know me.

Chapter 7: The Unique Blends

Maybe you wonder why there are times you just want to explore aimlessly with your friends. You scream for unexpected night outs, road trips and thrilling escapades. Then there are moments wherein you just want to shut people out. You yearn to be alone and enjoy the silence in a quiet beach, in an empty parking lot or simply in your bedroom. Perhaps this made you think that you're crazy; that yearning for silence and solitude is insane, but it isn't.

On the other hand, you might be uncomfortable with your own introversion. You feel odd and out of place. Being an introvert gives you the impression of being mentally ill. It drives you to want to "get out of your shell" and find a cure for being peculiar, but you couldn't find a way to do it, and if you did, it didn't feel right.

People congratulate you for finally "coming out of your shell", but the smile you put on is not the same as when you finish reading a well-crafted novel. It's not the same as when you have when someone spends time with you. You maintain the smile anyway because you think it's the cure for being an alien.

But the truth is it isn't.

There is no cure for introversion at all. It's just a matter of embracing and loving that exceptional part of you.

THE AMBIVERT FACTION

In the midst of introvert and extrovert scale, there are the ambiverts. They are the people who have learned to stretch their selves from their introverted side to the extroverted. They know how to even out being quiet and being loud. On some weekends, they hang out on their own. And on some, they can party all night with the world. They can exchange in small talks but somehow finds it somewhat insincere sometimes.

However, ambiversion is not something that comes naturally. The sole purpose of the introvert-extrovert concept is initially to ascertain whether a situation requires an extroverted or introverted response. Therefore, you have the choice in every situation whether you'll handle things inwardly or outwardly.

For example, if you need to work on an important book report, you need hours of solitude, blocking out any external stimulus and just get lost with your thoughts. On the other hand, if you need to present that report the next day, you have to consider external things like connecting with your audience and appearing interesting.

To sum this up, ambiversion is something that a person learns as he grows older in life. It's either an extrovert learns to adapt introvert abilities or an introvert learns to adapt extrovert abilities.

The Introverted Extrovert

"Introverted extroverts" are people who are dominantly extroverted but acquired the abilities of an introvert. As they grew up, life taught them to embrace the value of solitude. They are still outgoing and like being in the company of their friends, but they learned just how to empathize, to be extra sensitive and to ponder first before taking actions.

The Extroverted Introvert

In contrast, "Extroverted Introverts" are people who are dominantly introverts but acquired abilities of an extrovert. They are people who are willing to adjust to society, but they still need to be alone sometimes to recharge their energy.

BLENDING IT

The world grew up in a society that blossom on interaction. Everyone finds fulfillment in having friends, regardless if you're an extrovert or introvert. Every human being experiences this extraordinary bond with others, but don't form these bonds mainly by interaction or by internal stuff alone.

When you love someone, it's not enough to justify what you feel and think about that person, you must act on your feelings too. On the contrary, plain actions are not enough; they must come from a deep meaning from within yourself.

To put it simply, as a human, you are neither a pure introvert nor extrovert. Life is not about creating labels based on how you do things. It's about doing things to create labels. Your distinctiveness doesn't deserve to be simply categorized under labels that society created.

You should only use the labels, like those that the Myers-Briggs Personality Test suggests, as a tool to know yourself better, but don't let them limit you from becoming so much more. You are special. You are exceptional. There are things that only you can do for this world and nothing, absolutely nothing, should be a hindrance to that.

Chapter Five

Mastering the Art of Small Talk

Introverts tend to dread small talk. They worry that it will be boring, awkward, or that they'll run out of things to say. But in today's world, small talk is difficult to avoid. Cocktail parties, networking events, and even the line for coffee at work may require a brief exchange of pleasantries. You will be surprised to discover that small talk doesn't have to be painful.

Break the Ice

Though many of us find it kind of boring, small talk plays a big role in how we get along with others. Small talk is the gateway to connecting with people. There's this misconception that small talk is just a dumbed-down version of "actual talk" in which you dive deep, wax philosophical and get into the meat of a topic. Small talk is often synonymous with filler, fluff and inane banter. Choosing to stick to only deep conversation and avoiding small talk altogether is kind of like asking someone to marry you after a first date. Sure, you might strike gold and meet a person who is just as quick to jump the gun, and the two of you manage to make a connection, but these are exceptions. The vast majority of people are going to feel strangely uneasy every time they're around you. Begin at the beginning is all about small talk i.e. not over-sharing, not making any assumptions about the other person's opinions and beliefs, going easy until you can figure out how to not offend them. Small talk allows the parties in a conversation to get an initial sense of whether you are someone worth getting closer to. This is when, through subtle cues and body language, you can show a person that you are fun to be around, at the same time you get a feel for whether the energy is right. Small talk is essentially about allowing the parties in a group to judge each other without being too obvious about it. If you are shy, bad at small talk and feel out of place in a crowded room full of strangers, every new encounter is going to feel like a missed opportunity. Socially, mastering the art of light conversation can be a total game changer, and even if it isn't, at worst it'll make your life easier at all those networking events. Knowing how to initiate conversation, keep people interested and engaged is a super-skill that you can develop with practice. By learning a few simple techniques, you can polish your conversational skills and make a positive impression. Here are unique tips to master the art of small talk.

1. Reduce anxiety.

You may approach small talk with anxiety, ranging from slight apprehension to debilitating dread. To curb your anxiety, stay rational and positive. Tell yourself any of the following

The anxiety is coming from me and my beliefs, not the situation. I can do this.

What's the worst that can happen? If they don't like me, so what?

Labels don't define me. I'm an interesting, worthy person with a lot to contribute.

Everyone needs someone to talk to at networking events. If I strike up a conversation with that person, he or she will probably be glad to have someone to talk to.

2. Be purposeful.

Thoughts tend to be self-fulfilling. If you approach small talk with the belief that it will be dull and pointless, it probably will. Instead of dwelling on negative thoughts ("I'm awful at this," "I hate small talk," or "when can I go home?"), remind yourself that small talk isn't superficial. Small talk serves an important purpose – it helps build the foundation for authentic conversations and deeper relationships down the road. Think of small talk as the light appetizer before the main course, and approach it with renewed purpose.

3. Channel your curiosity.

Introverts tend to be curious people. They love digging deep, delving into topics that interest them, and learning what makes people tick. Channel your natural curiosity into small talk. When you ask "how are you?" or "how was your weekend?" approach the conversation with genuine interest. Carefully listen to the other person, and provide a thoughtful response. If you show true interest, you'll invite further discussion and set a positive tone for future interactions.

4. Ask questions.

Introverts tend to feel uncomfortable in the spotlight. They are often reluctant to disclose too much about themselves, especially to new people. So how can you start conversations and keep them flowing? The answer is simple – ask questions. By allowing the other person to take center stage initially, you can build your comfort level and test the waters before sharing your own thoughts. If you feel uncomfortable or fatigued mid-conversation, ask more questions and subtly turn the attention away from yourself. (But do not be tempted to let the other person do all the talking!) Add juicy tidbits. If you relentlessly pepper the other person with questions, it will feel like an interrogation. At some point, you must share a bit about yourself. Do not provide one-word, closed responses; these cut the conversation short. Instead, embellish your responses with juicy tidbits of information. By providing multi-faceted responses, you can provide "hooks" for the other person to continue the conversation.

For example: Question: "How are you?" Short response: "Fine." Better response: "Good, thanks. I'm getting ready for my vacation to England. It will be my first time in Europe, and I look forward to trying proper English tea."

Question: "Where are you from?" Short response: "Seattle." Better response: "I'm from Seattle. It doesn't rain all the time, and I enjoyed the amazing seafood and coffee. There are Starbucks on every corner."

5. Deepen the conversation.

The trick to making small talk successfully is observing your environment for conversation topics, then asking open ended questions about them. Start by scanning your surroundings for anything interesting – does the host have some strange pieces of furniture you could mention? Do they have awesome taste in art? Is the party located in a weird part of town? Does the person you are speaking to have a tan? A great haircut? Ask them an open ended question about it! These are the topics that make the best small talk fodder. Simple questions tend to elicit a one-word answer. Open-ended questions, on the other hand, can spark longer and richer discussions. Start with simple questions. After all, you don't want to scare the other person away. Open-ended questions can nudge the conversation into deeper, more authentic territory – where introverts tend to thrive. Consider some examples:

"Where are you from?", followed by "What is your hometown like? How is it different than here?"

"Have you attended events organized by this group before?" followed by "What did you think of today's presentation?"

6. Recognize cues.

Introverts are often misunderstood. Other people may interpret the introvert's reserved nature as snobbish, or they may find an introvert's deep passion for a particular topic to be too intense or serious. As an introvert, you can search for cues and learn to respond appropriately. For example, if the other person seems taken aback by your reserved nature, be sure to smile and express genuine enthusiasm in the conversation. Or if the other person starts to get fidgety while you're speaking at length on a subject, it's probably time to switch to another topic or wrap up the conversation. If you see that the other person is giving you short answers, it may be because they think you don't really want to hear the full story (this is especially true in formal networking situations where people expect a lot of empty but polite chatter). Just encourage them to continue; showing your interest, "I'd love to hear more about that." People LOVE to talk about themselves, so just let them. It's the easiest way of making small talk work.

7. Be kind to yourself.

Introverts are typically introspective souls who can concentrate for long periods of time. However, this gift can become a curse when you dwell on your own perceived faults and failures. If a particular endeavor didn't go well, you may replay the episode in your minds and berate yourselves for not doing things differently. If you botched up a conversation or wish you hadn't said this or that, take a few minutes to reflect and focus on your "takeaway" lesson for next time. Then simply let it go. Everyone makes mistakes. To accomplish anything worthwhile, you must be willing to fail many times (and occasionally look silly) before achieving success.

Don't be Outcome Dependent, Just Doing is What Matters. Be proud that you were able to go there first. That takes guts, and regardless of the outcome, it's a win. Most of all, don't try too hard. Often people think that they have to show their brilliance when they meet new people, actually, it's just the opposite. Be too erudite and you'll turn people off because it will make it hard for them to engage. When you first meet someone your job isn't to blow them away with your brilliant conversation skills. If you can, then great. But don't feel pressured to be Mr or Ms Profound with someone you barely know. In the early stages of conversation, your job is to send and to look for those subtle signals that tell you someone is comfortable with you, and open to moving beyond light conversation. The small talk phase is all about body language. People waste so much time trying to come up with interesting topics to talk about, but it almost doesn't matter what you say, as long as it's light, polite and politically correct. The conversation part of small talk is really just a very small part of the bigger picture. What matters more here is how you act, how warm you appear, how much charisma you exude and how interested you seem in the other person. The truth is small talk isn't supposed to be captivating, it's just an excuse for two people to throw empty words at each other long enough to get a good feel for each other's energy.

Chapter 8: Creative Strategies For Introverts To Get Out Of Their Shell

Sociability signifies the motive of desiring to be in the company of others. The need can be strong or weak, depending on one's personality. This is innate – life is all about connections and relationships. It is more than social networking, it is about face-to-face interactions and meaningful associations. There is a special exchange that happens in social interactions and relationships. Bonds are forged as joy and sorrow become shared.

But for the introvert, human connections and interactions do not come easy. Introverts would rather be the ones listening than doing the talking. They find it daunting to be in a room full of people they do not know. They would need to muster up extra courage to be present in an unfamiliar social setting.

If you are an introvert, you feel a lot of social anxiety. While there is nothing wrong with being reserved, you need to understand how social situations will benefit you. You can overcome this anxiety by applying the following tips:

Be creative and just do it.

Do not let your fear or apprehension get the best of you. It's time to broaden your boundaries.

To help you get out of your comfort zone, you can try by connecting with people through social media. It will help you transition to real-life contacts easier. Use Facebook, Twitter and other platforms to help you get to that level of comfortable familiarity with new people.

It may seem difficult in the beginning but think of social situations as an adventure. Studies show that when people see things as a challenge, they can cope better with anxiety. Push yourself to get out there. Take each social setting as an opportunity to grow and learn more. Smile at someone today, you never know what difference it will make in that person's life.

Relax.

Introverts prefer the comfortable; they rarely try something new. If you are invited to an event somewhere you haven't been, try this:

- Go to the venue ahead of time to familiarize yourself.

- Watch a favorite movie or something funny before the event so that you can relax your jittery nerves.

When you feel relaxed, you will exude happiness, confidence and a positive air around you. This will draw new people to you for conversation.

Start small.

You don't have to bring yourself out there and expect to know at least 100 people immediately. Take it slowly so you don't get overwhelmed. One step at a time, one stranger a day. Make simple, realistic goals.

Setting and achieving small goals will help boost your confidence and create a momentum of growth. When you are in a party or other social setting, make the effort to meet and talk with one person.

Don't be afraid to ask for help.

Introverts have at least on extroverted friend. If you have one, or two, ask for their help to overcome your social shyness. Let them bring you along to places and situations you wouldn't feel comfortable going on your own. With their naturally outgoing nature, you are bound to meet new people and be less intimidated.

Take note, though, that if you are with an extrovert friend, he or she may tend to take the spotlight and make you feel like you are a wallflower or a shadow. It doesn't matter; there's no reason to feel bad. Your goal is not to compete, but to build your confidence.

Embrace those nerves.

You may be scared, but go on and do it just the same. You can pacify a dull or awkward situation one step at a time. Being uncomfortable or nervous is normal;

there is nothing wrong with you. Keep in mind that everything takes practice, even socializing. You will get better at it over time.

Remember, it's not all about you.

While introverts are self-aware and introspective, they should also learn to put other people first. When you meet someone, ask him about himself and be interested in them. This will make them feel at ease and they will see you are a good conversationalist. Suppress the tendency to understand everything before you speak, you don't have to think too hard. Let conversations flow smoothly. Listen and answer as well. When you don't think too much about yourself, whether or not you are doing a great job at socializing, you will feel free and you will act more naturally and comfortably.

Drop the label.

So you are an introvert. This is one of the many different complex personalities that may be difficult to fully comprehend. Each person has his own traits, aptitudes, talents and personalities. But something is as powerful and that is how you perceive yourself. If you think of being an introvert as a limitation, stop right there.

Get out of the box that society has put you in. You don't have to conform. Drop the label: be creative, be empowered and be free to be yourself!

Chapter 9: Relationship And Communication Success

For this book, relationships refer to your friendships, family, professional and romantic connections. To have relationship and communication success, your self-concept must be congruent, solid, unwavering and positive. Calling yourself an introvert (or any predetermined social label) takes away personal accountability and actually limits your unlimited potential to manifest your life in exactly the way that you want. By doing so, the label will overshadow your true self, who is actually more adaptable and complex than you think.

By accepting personal accountability, you know that every direction your life goes is entirely up to you, and overall, your life is simply directed by the deepest motivation in you. Only YOU decide how your life goes. No condition, disorder or pre-determined set of traits will ever define who you really are. As mentioned earlier, you can rewire your brain and body to develop into any way that you want for as long as you nurture your health. Everybody has an ultimate genetic potential.

As you take the steps towards self-mastery, you will also begin to understand that you need other people to get there as well. Other people also need you to reach their best selves and potential. Consider this—what is your intention with every relationship that you want?

As you develop your inner strengths consider these attitudes as well.

When you are in a social interaction, do not simply be a passive spectator. Never underestimate your personal value. When you enter the lives of others, you are already playing a significant role. You are always directly involved in every conversation, and you have the ability to influence how every interaction goes.

Do not get stuck inside your own head, such as over-thinking of what to say next, being insecure about your looks, voice, words, and etc. Trying to "save face" and avoid embarrassment will only make you an incongruent person, and you will not be able to attract the people you truly want in your life this way. If you apply the steps in the previous chapter, your intuition and confidence will help you take more initiative and be significant in every interaction. The more in tune you are with your own emotions, and becoming comfortable with expressing them, the easier it will be to immerse in any social environment. And as you understand the minds of people more, you will have better empathy and receptivity to the feelings of others.

Being other-centered is a common sense idea that most of us "quiet types" actually underestimate. When you are working on being present in the moment, it is at this point that you must take your focus away from yourself, and into the world of another person. You can also train yourself to see every social interaction from a third person point of view.

You have to be genuinely interested in the emotions and experiences of other people. Always think of your own output. Think of going into every social interaction with an effort to add value to the lives of others, either by creating a good experience for them, making them feel good about themselves, giving them something, sharing something, or doing something that will add to or enhance their lives. Think of what you can give rather than what you can take from them. Be involved, even in small steps. Think of what this person or situation needs, based on your observation. And try to add to the situation. Always think in terms of adding, giving, and outputting. The common issue with introversion is the tendency to input so much that you can get stuck inside your own head. Do not absorb so much information and be overloaded in the process of introspection. Share what you learn, express them in ways that suit you.

Additionally, re-evaluate your self-concept, AND the concept of the social norm. Some people say be yourself, be your best self or be what is socially acceptable. However, it is all objective.

Throw away your concept of what is smart, or what is considered attractive. Stop trying to save face or "look impressive". More importantly, don't seek approval from others. You must see socialization as your opportunity to present your OWN unique view of the world, and understand that people truly want to know what you're all about. You are actually, truly enough. Your mind is an entire world in itself and it is fascinating to a lot of people, should you be happy enough to share it.

Every human interaction comes down to emotion and energy. It never matters what is SAID, or what is LOGICAL for a genuine connection to occur. Connection is focused on the emotional energy that is shared and transferred.

State transference refers to the idea that whatever you feel, they feel. If you feel good, other people will reflect. Create the mood energy in your head, and express it. Whatever you output will come back to you. and

The concept of creating good feelings within yourself, without depending on your environment, takes practice. But again, if your health and fitness is generally balanced, this will happen for you smoothly. Additionally, if your mind is stuck, then move the body! You have to move. Scream. Stretch. Do not stay static. This is what will create good energy within yourself, and it will translate to better emotions overtime. For example, before doing a presentation or going out on a date, you can instantly dissolve nervousness and mental blocks by doing a bioenergetics session and consuming foods that enhance your mood and energy.

You must build great abundance within yourself, to be able to ADD to other people's lives. You must always give first to eventually get what you want. The energy and intentions that you output will always come back to you. Know yourself strongly to know how MUCH you can give, and to WHOM you can give. Keep this up consistently and you will eventually attract the right people and relationships into your life.

Chapter 10: Building Skills In Functional Communication

Aside from talking about the things that you enjoy talking about, you should also build your skills in conversing with people for specific purposes. These skills will be mostly used in your professional life.

Practice common communications used at work

One of the biggest problems with introverts is that they think too much before starting a conversation. This can be a disadvantage at work where all people act as if they are in a hurry. If this is the case for you right now, you need to be aware of the areas of work that require communication. You should then practice these scenarios in your free time.

At work, either you need something from other people or they need something from you. If you do not like to talk to people, in general, you should practice making these interactions short. Go straight to the point when you are asking for something. If a person is making the conversation longer than it should be, you should practice politely dismissing him. Think of excuses ahead of time that will help you get out of conversations when you are in a hurry.

Practice small talk often

Most introverts think of small talk as a waste of time. You should consider however, that there are times when small talk is necessary. In the case of your professional life, for example, you need to use small talk so that you can meet new people to add to your network.

Let's take for example that you are in charge of a meeting. You arrived early in the conference room and you are there with one of your superiors. He is also waiting for the meeting to start. If you do not start a conversation, your boss may feel uncomfortable and he may not have a good impression of you. You should avoid awkward silences like those by using small talk.

Small talk is also useful when gathering information. Idle chatting puts people off their guard and makes them more open to giving information that they may deem as not important.

Small talks usually start with an opener. Either you or the other person starts the conversation by saying something that the other can relate to. How their day is going, for example, is a commonly used topic for openers. The opener is not meant to become the topic of the conversation. Rather, it should be used as a gauge whether the person is in the mood for talking or not. A person who is open to a conversation will add a comment to your opening statement even when the topic is not very interesting.

If the person responds favorably, you should then take the opportunity to introduce yourself. If the person is not interested in a conversation, he may provide a cold answer that does not invite conversations.

Practice job-related communication skills

In social settings, there will be several instances when you will be required to introduce yourself. In the professional world, this is also an opportunity to tell people what you do. Because you are just starting out, you should keep your introductions simple and straight to the point. Start with your name and what you do. You should then add a call-to-action. This is the part where you tell them that if ever they are in need of services like yours, they should call your number. As you say this, you should be handing them your calling card.

You should also practice pitching your company, product or services. Sales and new opportunities keep businesses alive. In the sales world, sales people are told to practice their elevator pitch. This pitch is usually 1-2 minutes long. It is called the elevator pitch because a competent sales person can deliver it in the duration of the elevator ride.

You should also practice delivering a presentation to people. Most introverts never hone this skill because they prefer to be at the sidelines. The fear of public speaking is also one of the most common fears for introverts and extroverts alike. However, if you want to succeed in your profession, you need to learn how to explain your ideas to people who matter. If you let other people explain your ideas, they may and will be given the credit for coming up with the idea.

Chapter 11: Tips For An Introvert. How To Survive Social Gatherings.

Even though introverts prefer time alone and would rather not attend social events there comes a time when they need to leave their comfort zone and mix with others. Here are some tips that will help even the most introverted individual be comfortable among others.

First, let's consider events and situations that can be avoided. Then we have events that shouldn't be avoided. Sounds simple right? The trouble is most introverts will find an excuse to avoid all events and are unaware there are times that their presence is required.

Situations to (optionally) avoid.

● Any weekly meetups. Some groups of people view a regular catch up at a local coffee house or drinkery as a must. Popular TV series are often based on these types of places (think Cheers, Friends and How I met your Mother) but you do not need to attend every meeting.

- Weddings of people you hardly know: When extroverts get an invite for any social occasion, they view it as an opportunity to meet new people. As an introvert, it is okay to turn down an invite to your former roommates' brother's wedding!

- Going to venues for dating purposes: The beauty of online dating sites means you can meet people without leaving the house. Of course, this does not mean there is anything wrong with traditional methods, but introverts have discovered a new way of meeting a potential partner.

Situations you shouldn't avoid.

- Networking events: You do risk a lack of progress in your career if you fail to attend every work event. Choose your events carefully and make sure there are people attending who you feel comfortable with.

- Special occasions for close friends and family: No matter how much you want to hide away it is imperative you attend

Christmas with family or close friends. Weddings and birthdays should also be shared with loved ones. Sometimes they will not accept your introvert ways as an excuse.

● Your own events: You may feel that the last thing you want to do is make a fuss over your special birthday or a work promotion. Well, you just have to realize that it is not all about you! Your friends and family want to share your celebrations and should be allowed to do so. The upside is that you do have a measure of control over the size of your party and the content. Remember, people only want to share stuff with you because they care.

When you do have to attend an event, here are a few tips that can help you survive the event.

● Come prepared with two conversation starters and an interesting story.

Default conversations that will help you engage other people are pets, holidays and travel, sports, recipes, and food and hobbies. You will find these topics will help get people talking and take the pressure off you.

You should always have a great story in your conversation armory. Something recent, amusing, inclusive and brief. Make sure you know what it is before the party!

● Wear a conversation topic

If you have an amusing tie or an unusual piece of jewelry you can break the ice with others when they ask you about it. Give people a reason to approach you and then expand on the conversation.

● Use your extrovert friends

Tagging a friend who makes conversation easily can help you piggyback into a social situation. Let your friend start the conversation and then sneak in and offer your input.

● Find a job to do

When an introvert enters a busy room all they see is a room full of people chatting away and having a great time. They believe that nobody is interested in what they have to say and feels totally isolated. We know that this is not a correct assessment of the situation but what can you do to feel less helpless?

If you see empty plates or glasses pick them up and head for the kitchen. If there is a plate of food sat on a table pick it up and head for groups of people. Food is a great icebreaker and you will feel you have a purpose. After a couple of minutes, you will feel more at home as you have a role to play.

- Power pose

Your posture can help you feel more confident. Simply stand with your legs apart and hands on hips for 2 mins and feel empowered. Think "superhero stance" and release your confidence.

- Check out a retreat

You can often feel that your energy has flagged before the evening ends and you need some 'me time". When you arrive at an event, scout out a possible bolt hole and use it when needed. It can be a patio, bathroom, kitchen or even your own vehicle. A few minutes away from the hubbub can provide much needed relief from external stimuli and allow you to catch your breath.

● Bookend your event with quiet times
Whenever possible spend time before a major event doing activities that soothe you. Read a book, have a Netflix binge or sit quietly. Just do whatever makes you calm. Energizing your mental batteries will help you cope with the noise and energy of the event ahead.

You should always allow a period of time to wind down following a party. Not only will you have space for yourself after a busy night, but you will have something to look forward to.

● Have an escape plan
As an introvert, you should always be aware of how you can leave if an event becomes too much for you. If you are relying on transportation home, then you will feel added pressure during the event.

You should ensure you have your own transport or a reliable alternative.

You should also avoid being anybody's ride home as this will put restrictions on when you leave. Having a degree of control will help you feel better about unfamiliar surroundings and company.

The key thing to remember is that people are interested in you and want to meet you! Your brain may be telling you that people really don't care and will not be remotely interested in you, but this is a fallacy! Put yourself out there and meet new people, it really is worth the effort.

Chapter 12: The Tips

WORK TIPS

Nailing the dream job

People think it's a no-brainer when an introvert is in line to be interviewed for a job along with a vibrant and chatty extrovert. Well, history and patterns have shown it's usually true, but the watchword is 'usually'. What can you do to turn this around as an introvert?

Harness the power of introversion!

We will look at a scenario, and how to apply our strengths to give the qualified introvert the upper hand.

First, we already mentioned that introverts are great listeners—better than the 'extros' for sure. Not only that, introverts are more observant and have the ability to keep their cool and maintain a professional demeanor.

When you have the option to exercise your power and choose a spot for an interview, bite back the urge to choose a spot ideal for you. We will see why...

If you want to get into a company and make an impact, you need to know how it works—no matter how much you've read about them. If there's the option of a social event and the option of a quiet restaurant or even library, pick the former. The social events give you the chance to do what you can do among them best—make crucial observations and apply your listening and learning skills. You may struggle with all the buzz and noise, but then again, introverts are great at maintaining composure when they want to. Do this well, and by the end of the day, you will be enriched with more info than the guy tasting every drink and laughing with everybody.

While we are at it, note this: make sure you go prepared. You know it may not be the best mind of place for you—all the noise and all. But you will be answering questions and exhibiting your intellectual abilities as well. Make no mistake, the jury won't be hiring you because you know how to party. First things first. So, outline your answers and questions well and perfect your routine before smiling to the sharks when the time comes. There may be some great extrovert successes like Mark Cuban, but think about it... Does that mean there are no introvert geniuses? Do you think the successful introverts want to be known? Oh, what about Zuckerberg and Bill Gates? Oh, there's Oprah Winfrey too!

Finding the right environment

Guess what? It isn't everywhere in the world that extroverts get the upper hand at work. Well, what we are saying is that there are certain environments where an introvert could easily thrive in some places in the world. If you are the kind of person who is looking wound up as a professional, or lonely, there are some countries where you can find solace. America isn't the best choice in the case, I bet. But particularly in northern Europe, you would find a great culture that doesn't depict the typical chaotic office culture synonymous to the American culture. In fact, the attitude of self-praise and a colorful competition isn't common and rather, space for the prosperity of the quiet professional is created.

Even though Sweden and the rest of Scandinavia are the places where an introvert may find most rewarding as far as work is concerned, the tendency to find highly-skilled professionals somewhat in hiding is also found in Russia.

Further down in Asia, particularly in countries like China, Japan, Korea and Vietnam, skill and self-worth isn't advertised by the verbal and vocal means that involves all the things the introvert loathes. Your competence practically has nothing to do with your personality or temperament.

So, if you are looking for a change in environment, these are not bad places to read about and possibly consider!

Oh, and do not forget that despite the popular knowledge of the more 'sociable' kind of employees making the mark, there are countless times when introverts stick to their cases and make outstanding careers for themselves. Whether in conducive environments like the computer software area where coding and more time with the computer is required—or uncomfortable jobs in a busy media office. The power is inside of you.

SCHOOL TIPS

First, we need to understand that the classroom can be a totally nightmarish place for an introverted student. But the thing is, it is not always as bad as it's made to be… If the student is 'prepared' for school, then he or she stands a greater chance of going through a day smoothly without having any trouble at all. Yes, you may freak out when it looks like the teacher is going to point at you or your little introverted child might dread the lunch bell, but all these can be dealt with by doing the right things:

Create a recharge zone:

The truth is, it is exhausting (especially for a younger introvert) to go through a full day of buzzing noise and events without having any avenue to cool off and reenergize their thoughts and systems. You are likely to be edgy when you are getting closer to the red line.

Even in school, valuable places can be found to mimic a niche where the introvert can successfully identify to recharge himself. A quiet reading zone or even a libraries is a great place for this. Having this available enables the introvert to tap into a resource that would energize as well as build confidence for the rest of the day for the student.

Focus on interests:

The introvert's confidence will be further peaked when they continually have more time and energy focused on what they thrive in or enjoy at school. In introverted kids for instance, you will be surprised to find they will actually man up in chatter once their favorite book or subject is laid before them. Shyness being associated with all introverts is a MYTH. Do not let people tag you with any stereotypical curse— an introverted student is never a weak or backward student, and given the opportunity, they prove it all the time.

A friend?

You may wonder what an introvert would do with a friend. In school, introverts of course are not too big on working in groups and all, but when they do, they are great observers, listeners and researchers. However, when they are 'paired' with like-minded people, it is easier for a bond to build between them and enhance academic and social productivity. Especially is kids, pairing is a great way to let the young introvert align with a companion. You would be surprised what two smart introverts can do! ☐

HOME TIPS? PLAY TIPS? NOT EXACTLY...

Rather than give straight forward tips for home, let's focus on some key aspects of family and relationships that introverts are keenly interested in: dating.

It actually frightens some people. First of all, you have to forget the external pressures that are eating at you. Friends and family will throw questions at you about dating and why and when— these relentless inquiries can be so exhausting!

However, you have to know these principles:

Do not rush to dates

Don't tell yourself you are psyched and then rush to three dates a week because you think you won't get another chance again. Why would you subject yourself to such torment? How are you harnessing your power of introversion by doing that?

Rather, the advice is this: DO go on dates, but only when you WANT to. Yes, it could be once a month or even longer, but never say never; you can't find love looking at yourself in the mirror all day—you definitely need to meet someone sometime.

Communicate— your way

Communication means the other person understands what you mean. While going on dates isn't top the list for any introvert, you will get there. When you do get to that point, let your preparation be as comfortable for YOU as possible, because it's the only way you can possibly be comfortable for the length of the night. Also communicate verbally and non-verbally with your date in a very frank and honest manner, so he or she knows what you are up to. There's a chance your partner may be smart enough to know how an introvert works, but not everyone does. So maybe, with some effort, let them know. Don't worry, they will do most of the talking anyway, and by now, you know you have to master the art of staying composed and listening.

You are the one to let your partner understand that to the introvert, proximity means much more than talk. This golden piece of knowledge somehow has to travel to the other person—then you could have a fun time!

Chapter 13: Social Anxiety

"Shy people fear negative judgment, while introverts simply prefer less stimulation; shyness is inherently painful, and introversion is not. But in a society that prizes the bold and the outspoken, both are perceived as disadvantages."

Susan Cain

The Shy Introvert

As this chapter's opening quote says so well, being shy is not the same as being an introvert.

You might be a shy introvert, but you might not be shy at all. You just may keep to yourself.

Let the label go and be yourself.

The Anxious Introvert

Introverts have social anxiety?

Maybe yes, or maybe no.

While it is not uncommon for an introvert to experience social anxiety, not all do, and the degree certainly varies by person and situation.

There is a tendency for anxiety to build up over time. An introvert experiencing social anxiety may cause others, or even themselves, to begin to think of these to be one and the same, but it does not have to be this way.

The Easiest Way for Introverts to Reduce Anxiety

This one may surprise you, but it is good news.

As an introvert, you may find that your greatest stresses are the result of trying to live your life according to what extroverts like.

Workplaces, meetings and social settings can be loud, lack privacy and leave no time to think. The things that introverts need to survive and thrive (e.g. quiet, time to reflect and time alone) are often missing from these environments.

If you create quiet, privacy and time alone each day, you may find yourself less anxious.

Yes, it can be as simple as that.

If it sounds too simple, try it.

If you need more, that's ok, but it's a foundation.

Expecting yourself, as an introvert, to not experience stress in loud places where you get no time to think, let alone to be alone, is unreasonable.

What Else You Can Do

Here are a few other things you can do that may help you reduce your anxiety:

Get enough sleep.

Eat well and avoid too much caffeine.

Arrive early at events.

Have an exit plan.

Give yourself permission to leave.

Take a time out.

Remind yourself to breathe.

Focus outward on someone else, versus inward on yourself.

Find one person that you can talk to and ask them a great question that will keep them talking.

Butterflies - Exercise

How do you make your butterflies fly in formation?

Take a few minutes to write down the things you currently do to reduce your anxiety.

Put big ☐ stars ☐next to the ones that make the biggest difference.

Draw some butterflies if you wish.

Now add to your list the suggestions from this chapter that you would like to try.

Draw some caterpillars if you wish.

These are your future butterflies, and you can teach them to fly in formation.

As we wrap up this chapter, here are a few helpful caveats to keep in mind:

Give yourself permission to take a break or step away from any situation that causes you to feel anxiety.

Planning ahead by preparing yourself for events and activities can help to decrease your anxiety.

Chapter 14: Introverts In The Business Scene

There are a lot of strategies to become successful. Many don't only pertain to introverted people, but to the whole demographic who wants to enter the business world. Before anything else, you need to silence all those voices that keep telling you that an introvert isn't the ideal type of employee in the very competitive, harsh, and cynical environment that is the business world. If you often see yourself cowering in fear or opting out of the organization or company that you're in, this is not necessarily because of your introversion, but perhaps a wrong choice of business path.

Introverts find it challenging to move around the workplace in terms of voicing their ideas and being assertive in opportunities. This often leads to introverted people in the corporate scene feeling left out and misunderstood. The common mistake when there are workers like this is to label or define them unfairly. In some cases, they are deemed to be weak, passive and lack confidence. Most of the time this isn't true. There are introverts who aren't really shy but just don't feel the need to actually get their ideas out there. It's not a shortage of belief in themselves or in their thoughts; they would just rather keep it inside their minds and see it only as a chore to explain themselves to others.

The extroverts, on the other hand, get challenged in this type of situation and often come up with positive ideas and forward-thinking risks, which they will waste no time in sharing. The drawback to it this is how extroverts are then defined as people who talk first and think later.

When it comes to networking, despite popular thinking, introverts do handle meeting new people well. In the conventional sense, they are good at interacting with a person one-on-one rather than in groups. And when introverts meet new people, they don't just build bridges, but also build a very strong foundation for relationships.

If you are an introvert and you're wondering how you can survive networking seminars or events, just remember not to get in your own way. Approach the situation as you would normally do when you meet with your friends or a best friend. Don't look at people as assets, rather see them more intimately, as opportunities for future friends. Don't let yourself get to a point where everything you're doing or saying doesn't feel normal to you anymore.

Chapter 15: The Introverted Life

Every time I've done a Myers-Briggs Type Indicator inventory (MBTI), the bar indicating that I'm an introvert is so long that you'd almost think the paper ran out of space. I'm a rare MBTI type (INFP--less than 5% of the population: introverted, intuitive, feeling and perceiving). Dealing with that boundary between my reality and what the rest of the world knows as normal is one of the challenges I've been grappling with all my life. Reading, fortunately, offers us one of those windows--and it's especially useful to introverts like me because it doesn't require conversation.

Right now I'm reading a book on Eat, Pray, Love, and I've just finished reading about her months in an ashram in India. During her time there she came to understand the value of silence and--despite her natural, talky extraversion--yearned to transform herself into the Quiet Girl in the

Back of the Temple. It was fun to read her description of the mystical and mysterious qualities she sees in quiet people.

The book never gets off the ground because the ashram, recognizing her unique gifts, assigns her to a job that requires someone who's "social and bubbly and smiling all the time." And that's something that (in my fantasies, at least) often happens to extroverts: Being affirmed and rewarded for being themselves. Introverts like me, on the other hand, often have the horrifying experience of opening their mouths and seeing nothing come out. Or something lame. But then why would I want to be an introvert, let's explore that question: What, exactly, is enviable about introverts? Here's my list:

1. We learn early that effort is necessary. Unlike extroverts, with their easy charm, we have to struggle to make small talk and build friendships. Imagine what it's like for an introvert to go for a job interview, join

a new club, or go to a party or reception. Introverts tend to be disciplined people with a higher-than-average ability to concentrate.

2. We're not always shy. Find a topic that interests us, and we'll astonish you with our vitality. I'm a lifelong teacher who thrives on the interaction with a large group of people--as long as I'm talking about something I care deeply about.

3. Spontaneity doesn't work for us. Because introverts have to process everything internally, we respond slowly and awkwardly when we're put on the spot. If you're planning a big surprise for your favorite introvert, here's some heartfelt advice: Don't do it.

4. We have good social skills. I know this sounds strange: If social gatherings are so uncomfortable for introverts, why would we be good at them? The answer is that we can't just do what comes naturally, so our social skills tend to be highly tuned.

Introverts quickly learn that they have to prepare ahead of time for social events:

Who's going to be there? What might be going on in their lives? Can I get some follow-up questions ready about the topics we talked about last time? What's been going on in my own life lately that I can talk about? What current events can I bring up?

5. We know how to build connections and trust. Unlike extroverts, who tend to chatter away without checking out their companions' facial expressions and body language, introverts constantly look for feedback. And we're good at picking up conversational clues--a trip you mentioned, a movie you saw or book you read.

6. We tend to have good manners. You won't find us talking on and on about a third person you don't know--something my extrovert friends often do. We might be slow to find a topic to talk about, but we're thinking about doing it.

And that's what introversion is like. How can you help your introverted friends and acquaintances? First, never say "You don't remember me, do you?" If we don't know you well, remind us who you are, and toss out some conversational clues for us to grab. Second, be open to learning from us (something we do all the time as we struggle to learn how to function in an extroverted world). Most important, remember that internal processing is important to us, and give us a few extra seconds to do it.

Chapter 16: What It's Like To Date An Extrovert

How hard is it for an introvert to build a romantic relationship with an extrovert or vice versa? There are many challenges for both sides in this type of relationship. Yet it just might be the most rewarding once you break through the initial barriers. As you know, I am successfully married to an extrovert, and I would not have it any other way. I was attracted to my spouse when we met because he seemed to be high energy, aggressive, passionate and intelligent.

Remember the continuum we discussed earlier? Remember that someone could be 80% extrovert and 20% introvert. Maybe you are comfortable with an extrovert who is 70-30 instead of 80-20. Maybe you need even less of an all-out people person and want a 60-40 instead. Get a sense of how far to the extrovert side your date is before you get too involved. Still dating an extrovert when you are an introvert is not easy.

There are some plusses to dating an extrovert if you are an introvert. You might be able to calm down the extrovert, and he might be able to bring you a little out of your shell. You can make an extrovert happy when he can go out with friends, because he does not have to entertain or be with you all the time. On the other hand, when he has worn himself out with all his activities, they can rest in your space and know that you will welcome them in.

On the other hand, it is very easy for introverts to feel invisible when they are dating an extrovert because all of the attention goes to the extrovert. There is also the potential danger of being abandoned in social situations to take care of yourself, while your extrovert is gone to socialize with just about everyone in the place. We all know this is about the worst thing you can do to an introvert. So there are advantages and disadvantages to dating an extrovert. Obviously for myself, I found the advantages to far outweigh the disadvantages.

Even when I did find myself alone at a social event because Tom was off socializing, I could usually find a nice quiet spot, preferably outside, to sit alone and gather my thoughts for a few moments. Even more often, I would glance around when I found myself alone, and find another introvert who had been abandoned by his extrovert wife. I would strike up a conversation with this kindred soul, and we would be fine until our talkative extroverts returned to claim us.

Advantages of Dating an Extrovert

Often it is exciting, invigorating and a great experience to date an extrovert. They have a lot to share with you.

You might learn to be less introverted in a relationship with an extrovert. You might learn to make small talk or be more spontaneous, that might help in your work environment.

Allows the extrovert to bring you out of your shell a little while you use your calming energies to slow him/her down a little. The extrovert can rest with you when they are worn out, and you can get out and socialize with her/him. Being there for each other means your extrovert needs to understand that you might feel abandoned or invisible at times.

Do's and Do nots When Dating an Extrovert

It will take a lot of dialogue and compromise between the two of you to make it work.

Start out in a small group or try activities where you are active and not put in a position where you have to have a lot of "small talk"

Even if you do not have a lot of small talk to do you should still plan for some. If the scenario is one in which you have already agreed to a date with an extrovert and you know there will be some small talk – plan it out. The extrovert is going to be by nature more spontaneous than you, so there is no shame in planning out the initial conversations you want to have. Make a list of ideas and some questions you might want to ask your date. Remember you are dating an extrovert and if you get them talking you can do what you do best and that is listening. Let the extrovert do most of the talking.

Go on trial runs with a family member or friend. Make these trial runs just like the real date. Follow the topics you have rehearsed and have your friend or family member just taking the conversation wherever they feel it goes. Before I met my spouse I had a date with another extrovert. A friend suggested this technique, and it worked well for me.

This way you can get comfortable with the conversation going off topic and starting a new topic before the old one was finished, and maybe even going back to the original topic. Doing this several times before your actual date with an extrovert will help you gain confidence and comfort with the situation. It worked for me.

Make sure you are well rested – get enough sleep before your date with an extrovert. Be sure you have had the quiet time you need to re-energize yourself before you go out and give up your energy. Also make sure you have the time and space to re-energize again after the date. When I first met my husband and started dating him, I knew how energized he was and how much being with him would drain my energy. So if possible I made sure I had time set aside after the date to re-energize myself.

Let your extrovert talk and you can listen, using your introvert skills to get to know him/her better. Just remember there has to be some smaller amount of time when your date listens to you.

If you are not comfortable talking much then go on dates that require you to do something physical rather than something like a dinner date. Go for a bike ride, to a movie, or even a double date.

Compromise on your second or third date and do something a little more oriented to your extrovert. Then plan a stay at home movie for the following date. This way you will build on the strengths that both of you have in the relationship and build the rapport between you.

On the other hand, as an introvert you might want to go to someplace quieter than the norm – like a coffee shop – but that will require you to talk more so it is a tradeoff.

As an introvert, you are excellent at establishing rapport. Use all your listening skills to establish rapport in the first three or four dates. By then you should be clicking on all cylinders if this is going to grow into a long term relationship.

I knew at the end of my second date with the extrovert I dated before my spouse that it was not going to work. On the other hand, it was about the same place in the relationship with my spouse that I knew I wanted to know more about him.

Do not try to change each other – just respect the differences. Even though there might be major differences between you and an extrovert, do not try to make the extrovert into your image as an introvert. Let him be himself and use your introvert skills of listening and empathy to learn to understand the extrovert on a deeper level.

Beware of certain traits in your extroverted date. You expect him to be a talker, but if you NEVER get to talk then this is not the right person. How do you feel when you are with him? Comfortable or overwhelmed? Calm or panicky? Pay close attention to what your body is saying about your extroverted date. Finally, be sure your extrovert is as much of a giver as you are. If you have to ask her to be romantic but she expects you to be, perhaps this match is not going to work.

Make sure your extrovert understands that you need quiet time and solitude – no matter what – and it does not mean you do not want to be with him. It means you do not want to be with anyone during that period of time. Secondly make sure your extrovert understands that you cannot be made over into an extrovert and shouldn't be. Love me as I am or find someone else should be your message.

Finally, the extrovert you are dating needs to understand that you might not say much, but you mean what you say. If you say "I love you" that is forever even if you never say it again.

Chapter 17: 30 Ways To Know If You're An Introvert

30 Ways to Know If You're an Introvert

Introverts and extroverts are not better than the other but there is an undeniable distinction between them. So which of the extremes do you fall into? To find out if you are among the minority personality, below is a list that you can check to see if one or more situations apply to you in your everyday encounters.

1. You wish you could put everything you need within the confines of your home so you won't have to commute and bump into people.

2. There's a slight panic build up when people stay in your office after you've said your formalities such as greetings and polite one-liners.

3. You stop when you notice that someone is watching you do your work.

4. You've thought about putting up the words "Busy. Kindly move along." on your office door.

5. "Never show a work in progress" is one of your mottos.

6. 4 hours is still not enough time to start a conversation with the person sitting next to you.

7. In anticipating performing a task, you repeat the steps in your head like a loop.

8. There's that compulsion to focus and complete the task at hand or goodbye good night sleep.

9. He just helped you with your work. You ask yourself, "Why? Why? Why?!"

10. You dread working in a group.

11. You wonder why people argue over discussions when the fun part is listening.

12. When in a group setting, the possibility of being picked out to ask for your opinion is making you anxious.

13. Often, you wish you can stamp the words "Leave me alone" on your forehead.

14. You are not easily influenced by others when it comes to your work or attitude because you know you are doing a great job and feels contented.

15. Somebody got a flu at the office. Better sanitize constantly and drop by the doctor's office for some shots. You don't want to risk it.

16. On most days, you think other people ate a bowl of stupid for breakfast.

17. Sometimes they think you're slow because you don't react to inquiries on reflex.

18. A night out with colleagues seems like such a waste of a perfectly good night.

19. After only 15 minutes in a party, you tell yourself, "I want to go home now."

20. You hate being called "shy" but people seem to call you that constantly that it's almost synonymous to your name.

21. There's a company trip set in another city. You look forward to the long drive alone.

22. Long wait in the bank? Perfect time to catch up on your reading.

23. You hate small talks but you'll talk to a dear friend about what life means.

24. People invited to your special events can all be written on a post-it.

25. You think voice mail is sent from heaven.

26. Storm? Snowed in? Awesome! You can stay in the whole day!

27. You are very proud of the savings in your bank account and the properties you've accumulated but you do not boast it.

28. You tire yourself with your own thoughts.

29. There's a journal near your bed.

30. Losing in touch with a "friend" makes you feel relieved.

Time to go home.

"Great work today, Kate."

Would have been better if we finished. You just kept jumping from one thing to another like a crazy person. But she smiled. At least she's going home.

"See you Monday, Matthew."

He looked a little offended. "It's Marcus."

Home.

She's lying face down on her carpet again. She feels terrible.

This may not have been the normal day she was expecting. How horrible of her. Matthew. Marcus. Matthew is not Marcus. If she jumbles the letters in "Marcus" it won't get her "Matthew". Not in a million years! She's supposed to be smart.

Ring. No.

Ring. No.

Voice mail. Yes.

"Kate, it's your mother. Do you remember me? We're still having lunch on Sunday, don't forget. Stop locking yourself in your apartment. It's not good and very off-putting. Can you answer the phone, please? What on earth do you use it for if not to talk to your mother? I wish you'd go out and meet people."

I wish you'd press "end call" again. And I hate people, Mom.

The line ended. Finally.

Leave me alone to wallow in my mistakes. Why didn't I care enough to know his name? Why can't I be like Bessie? No, wait, I take that back. I don't want to be like Bessie. All that talking to people and going out every night. I'm exhausted just thinking about it.

Chapter 18: Overcoming Shyness And Improving Your Social Skills

Most of the time, the reason why introverts do not socialise much is not that they would rather be alone all of the time, but rather, they do not know how to compose themselves in front of others. In other words, they are socially awkward and shy. The good news is that you can get rid of your shyness and you can learn how to socialise; you were not born with these traits, you can change these things within yourself.

Here are some simple tips that you can use to rid yourself of your shyness and become more sociable. Keep note though, the changes within you will not take place immediately; it will take a bit of time so you should be patient and do not give up hope.

Practice

Just like any other skill, you can learn to become more sociable through practicing.

This may seem too extreme, but the only way for you to practice socialisation is to jump right into it. When you meet new people and actually have conversations with them, you will start dismantling your prior belief that you do not need other people to be happy. The more people you interact with, the more you will learn how to read and attune yourself to them, which makes for a better conversation.

You may think that you are avoiding socialisation because you do not have passable social skills, but continuing on your current path will not do anything to change things. This may seem like a veritable Catch-22, but it is not as hard as you think it is.

Interact with Sociable People

One of the best and easiest ways to become a more socially awesome person is to model yourself on others. This is actually easy, you just need to talk to people who have excellent social skills; you do not even have to do too much work, they will make the entire interaction easy for you, that's how good they are. All you have to do is observe how they carry themselves throughout your conversation. You need to take note of their mannerisms, the tone of voice they use, their hand gestures, absorb everything that you can. When you get home, go and try out the things that you've learned through your observations; of course, not all of them will feel natural for you, but there will surely be one or two that will feel right. Once you find a couple of "moves" that seems like a right fit for you, try them out on other people and take note of their reactions to your new repertoire of social skills. If you feel like things are not going the way you thought they would, adjust yourself accordingly.

Pick A Specific Skill and Work On It First

There are many different kinds of social skills, so many in fact that trying to master them all at once is not a good idea. The best approach to learning social skills is to pick one and focus all your energy into improving it first before working on another one.

You do not actually have to become a full-blown extrovert, you just need to learn the kinds of social skills that you want to learn. Since you are an introvert, you do not really like to become the centre of attention. In this case, you only need to learn how to initiate communication, engage in small talk, and other small, yet important social skills. For someone like you, learning how to talk with another person without feeling nauseated is already enough to make you content.

Chapter 19: How To Initiate Conversations

The best way for an introvert to deal with his chronic anxiety is to learn to talk to new people. To make a change with what you are doing now, you should be the one to start conversations with them.

How to develop the habit of starting conversations:

Do not do small talk, have a goal when communicating

Introverts hate making small talk. When you talk with someone, you always need to have a goal. A goal separates a meaningful conversation from small talk. The goal does not need to be important. However, you need to have a reason for starting a conversation.

In settings that are more professional the goals are more obvious. Sometimes you need to communicate to get the job. You may also need to communicate to build rapport with coworkers or clients. Some people are highly skilled in transactional communication. These types of communication have goals like closing a deal, making a sale or convincing others to do a specific set of actions.

Communication goals however can extend beyond the professional realm. Your conversation goal could be as simple as to kill boredom or to find out more about the other person. For instance, when you meet someone new, and you happen to like that person, you can find out if you share interests by asking questions.

Make your goals short and simple

When you decide to talk to someone new, you should instantly think of a goal for the conversation; don't make your goal too complicated because it will only make you more anxious.

Make your goal short and simple so you can easily attain it. Short and simple goals are easy to remember even when you are in the middle of a conversation. If you suddenly run out of things to say, just go back to your goal. By thinking of your goal in these instances, you will not sound like you are just prolonging the conversation to avoid the awkward silence.

You do not need to talk to everyone around you

Most introverts feel pressured in a social setting because they feel that everyone is looking at them. They compare themselves to extroverts who usually get all the attention.

If you are in a social setting, do not think too much of what other people think of you. Instead, you should focus on only the interesting people in the group and start talking to them. Let your goal guide you on your decision on who to talk to.

If your goal in the social event is to gain more connections of potential clients, you should talk with the person who may become interested with what you are offering.

Make a list of the things that interests you

People usually run out of words to say when they aren't familiar with the topic of the conversation. You can avoid these scenarios by only bringing up things that you spark your interest. If you like movies, start talking about the latest movie you watched. If you love gardening, you can bring that topic up too. By being aware of the topics that you are knowledgeable about, you will be confident in starting conversations.

Take note of how you start your interactions with your current friends

As mentioned earlier, most introverts already interact consistently with their own circle of friends. This is a sign that they can communicate effectively if they are comfortable with people they are talking to.

When interacting with your circle of friends, pay more attention on how the interaction starts or how they happen. These details in the communication process are so subtle that we usually miss them. You should observe the interactions and look for certain patterns.

For instance, find out who always starts the conversations. You should also observe how and when you usually start participating. Do you only speak when the other person asks a question? Do you initiate the interactions with your friends?

If you are the initiator, you can simply apply your communication style with other people outside your circles. You can easily start communicating with other people if you just act normal. If you already know how to start interactions, you do not need to change your personality just to become socially acceptable.

If you are just the participant and never the initiator, you need to start initiating interactions within your group of friends. By doing so, you practice your communication skills with the people you are comfortable talking with. You will also build confidence to start conversations with people outside your circle. You can then apply the things you learn when interacting with people outside your circle.

Master the art of questioning

Knowing when and how to ask questions is a useful skill to have when talking to new people. When you ask questions, you show the people you are talking to that you are interested in their lives. It is an easy way to make a person open up.

Asking the right questions also allows you to gauge the willingness of the other person to communicate. When you ask a person something and they give an extensive answer, this means that they are willing to talk with you. If the person you talk to does not feel like talking, they will let you know through the length of their answers, their attitude when answering and the non-verbal cues that they are sending your way. When you find someone who is not willing to open up, that is a sign to exit the conversation and find someone else to talk to.

In the best-case scenario, you can build rapport with a person through questioning. A person skilled in asking questions can carry a conversation without talking too much. They allow other people to talk. They are comfortable with being the listener.

Have an exit strategy

A conversation usually becomes awkward when both parties do not know how to end it. You can avoid the awkwardness of long conversations by having an exit strategy. There are multiple ways to do this. You can simply tell the person you are talking to that, you have another meeting to go to. In the office, you can say that you have a lot of work to get back to. There are multiple excuses that you can use to get out of a conversation but it is better if you use an honest and valid excuse rather than a lie.

Learn the common courtesies in the new group of people

When interacting with a new group of people, be mindful with the informal courtesies that they are practicing. This is very important especially when communicating with a group from a different cultural background. If a specific action is potentially offensive, do not do it. You should also be careful when talking about sensitive topics like politics, religion and social issues important to the group.

Chapter 20: Practical Help

This chapter tackles real-life questions from introverts and provides answers.

"I feel like my introversion is keeping me from making the most of my life. Is there a way to change this nature and be more outgoing?" ~George, 17.

Questions about how people can make the transition from introversion to extroversion is an exciting angle that many people want to explore. The question is, is that even possible? In previous chapters, it's been noted that being an introvert solely depends on how dominant your introversive traits are when compared with your extroversive traits. Scientifically, introversion can be genetically inherited. So, some introverts are just naturally predisposed to their traits. Nevertheless, those who were born as introverts may still display qualities of extroversion.

What if George was born an introvert? How would you propose he handles the situation?

It doesn't really matter if George was born as an introvert or if his environment and culture required him to become one. He is still just as introverted. The actual problem is what could have caused this desire to be more outgoing. Many things could have happened over time. A change in environment, new friends, a new taste of affection, peer pressure, new goals, family issues, religious views and teenage dreams could make an introverted George want a change in personality. There are times when people seem to want a quick and drastic change, but what they truly need is an intentional improvement in the status quo. With the following tips, perhaps you'll start to understand that getting hold of yourself is what truly matters at the end.

Tips to help stay in control of your introversion

Think your thoughts out loud

Sharing is love. Everyone feels loved when given a gift. You can give of your time, energy and words. Mostly, your words are the smallest but strongest gifts you can give to anyone. Let your thoughts out even if it seems odd and feels weird at first. In that way, you can have a good edge over the strong influence of solitude. You know what is always intriguing? Things that seem quite out of the ordinary. If your thoughts and imaginings are perceived by you as bewildering, don't shut them inside, instead talk about them. If you feel empathetic about a situation or toward someone, be sure to head over and offer a listening ear. Don't feel responsible for the incident. Letting out honest words from your heart and hearing yourself say them out loud might just be the reassurance you need to keep you steadfast in all the ways that you are striving to do better. Know that your thoughts will only keep lurking deep inside of you for as long as you shut them in.

"I'm the only introvert in a family full of extroverts. I love them but they sap my energy. They're always hosting events, throwing parties or inviting me to one event or the other. They don't take no for an answer and it makes me resent them. Sure, sometimes I enjoy spending time with them but most times, I'm moody and tired when I have to go out for these events." ~ Sylvia, 22.

Introverts are like fireflies. One second, they sparkle while the next moment the light goes dim and eventually turns off. The fact that your moods seem to be like a car trying to accelerate on a dirt road horribly filled with potholes shouldn't cause you to feel totally out of control. There's no better way to deal with a family of extroverts than educating them on why you need time to recharge. Family is important, try to find a balance between your private time and socializing.

Find, expand and strengthen your social ties

"A few years ago, I couldn't keep up with social calls and gatherings. Later on, I realized that I needed to be there for people I truly cared about. To show that I cared, I had to keep up the effort to answer their invitations. I started with the most exciting ones. Weddings! Later, I began attending get togethers, parties and picnics. Then, it just happened. I developed an interest in social outings. It did take some time though." ~ Williams. 32

As an introvert, flexing your social muscles requires intense determination and a strong will. What if you have no social circle at all? Realistically, that's almost impossible. There is always family and a few friends. Truth is, you can't be there for everyone. Just in case you ever decide to expand your social circle, don't go running after anyone that seems cool. Start off with family, neighbours, workmates and maybe your favourite superstore attendants. Expanding your social circles shouldn't be a game, you need to want to care for those you'll be meeting with.

A broad smile accompanied by the mention of their name with no undertones to your greeting will get your neighbors and colleagues interested in talking with you. Also, do your best not to forget people's names. People will take you seriously when you remember little details about them. Go out more. Don't wait to be invited, take the initiative and take a couple of friends out for a movie or a drink. If at first you feel worried about testing the waters of the extrovert world, you can always bring your social circle home and try to enjoy the comfort that comes from being around people who care about you.

Overcoming the drawbacks of introversion won't come easy, but it will definitely make your life more meaningful if you at least try. Remember, you're not trying to lose your personality, you're only trying to keep it under control and live beyond its so-called restrictions.

Chapter 21: Use The Right Words

One of the reasons why introverts are often afraid to ask for alone time or decline invitations is that they are afraid that what they say could offend their friends and loved ones. After all, since most people are extroverts or fall more to the side of the introvert-extrovert scale, it might be difficult for them to understand why you are saying no to spending more time with them.

For the sake of the introvert's emotional health and peace of mind, however, it is important for them to set boundaries. But oftentimes, they don't know how to communicate what they need and so they end up keeping silent, which causes inner frustration to build up that can hurt their personal relationships in the long run.

Here are some suggestions on how to use the right words to set boundaries and deal with various social situations:

Avoid lying as much as possible. If you are just dealing with acquaintances, then it is okay for you to make up the generic "other commitments" so you can say no to going out with them. With people you are closer to, however, you should try to tell the truth as much as possible, since when they learn that you are lying, it could prove more offensive than saying 'no'.

Make it about you and not about them. One of the reasons people feel offended when you say 'no' to invitations for social events is that they feel you are saying no to spending more time with them. Of course this is not the case. You know that you do like being with them, but you just have to take time out.

Thus, when you decline invitations, make sure to phrase them in such a way that the person you are talking to knows that it is because you need to go home because you're tired or need to decompress. For instance, you can try: "I would say yes but I'm afraid I'll fall asleep and embarrass myself" or "I've had all the fun I can handle for one night".

If you are backing out of a group event, make sure to let the person know you are willing to spend time with them, but on a one-to-one basis. If you're invited to a group event but feel that it is wrong for you, you should make it clear to the person you're dealing with that it is the event that you are declining, not spending time with them.

So when you say no, try saying things like: "I'm not comfortable with large groups; let's schedule lunch instead" or "I'll pass but maybe we can get together at another time?"

One thing you should realize, however, is that for some people, whatever you say can be construed wrongly. So you should also prepare yourself for the inevitable times when somebody does take offense, no matter how carefully you phrase your words. When they do, you should make sure that you do not internalize their taking offense or take it personally. Remember that, in this case, it is about them and not about you.

Chapter 22: Misconceptions And Myths

"Whatever kind of introvert you are, some people will find you 'too much' in some ways and 'not enough' in others." ~ Laurie Helgoe

There are a lot of misconceptions about introverts

like they are antisocial, unfriendly, shy or lonely, but in many cases, being an introvert can actually be an asset. Introverts are people who get their energy from spending time alone, it's kind of like a battery they recharge, and then they can go out into the world and connect really beautifully with people. Introverts take longer time to process information than extroverts, this is actually because they process more thoughtfully than extroverts do, they take extra time to understand ideas before moving on to new ones.

While we are all often flooded with messages that we need to speak up and stand out in order to be successful, introverts can actually achieve even more if they hone their natural strengths. People may think introverts are small, but they have a universe inside their mind. Introverts like saying the most with the least amount of words, when it comes to word economy introverts are the best economists. They may talk less, but they speak a lot with their actions, even their silence speaks more than the most talkative people in the room, and yet it is meaningful. It is advised that if you don't have anything valuable to speak it's better to keep quiet and let people think that you are an idiot than speak up and prove them right. I believe that originality thrives in seclusion where it is free of outside influences beating upon us to cripple the creative mind. I feel being alone is the secret of invention, when someone is in their solitude that is when ideas are born and they come out effectively. Here are some of the benefits of being an introvert:

they are good listeners; introverts are naturally adept when it comes to actively listening. Introverts tend to be the friend or colleague who someone can call when they are upset or when someone has good news to share; introverts will be able to listen and be with them in that, without turning it around. Extroverted people are more inclined to jump into a conversation before fully processing what the other person has said. Not because they areselfish or don't care, but because they process information interactively. I am alarmed about our society, when being alone is considered suspect; when one has to apologize for it, make excuses, hide the fact that one practices it like a secret hobby.

You don't have to be an extrovert to change the world, neither you need to be an autocrat to do so; it can be done in a gentle way, you can shake the world with your ideas. Introverts process information internally. That skill allows them to hear, understand and provide carefully considered insight when they do respond. They think before they speak because introverts typically feel less comfortable speaking than they do listening, they choose their words wisely, we only speak when we have something to say, and so there is a higher chance that we will have an impact with our words. That being said, introverts may take a little too long to formulate their thoughts before sharing them — especially in fast-paced business settings. The skill of choosing words wisely is just as beneficial online as it is in person, so choosing what to write in an email, is important too.

Introverts are observant, in addition to their superior listening skills, introverts possess what I consider a "superpower": their observation skills. We notice things others might not notice because they are talking and processing out loud. Although it may look like they are just sitting quietly during a meeting, introverts are actually soaking in the information that's being presented and thinking critically. The typical introvert also uses their observant nature to read the people and the room. They are more likely to notice the body language and facial expressions of the people, which makes them better at interpersonal communication. Introverts are like a very well maintained and contented website which takes time to load; there usually is a lot of cool stuff however most of the people don't want to wait for them to open up; in contrast the extroverts are kind of pop up advertisements, they will come and try to interact even if you are not interested at all.

Introverts are especially skilled at noticing introvert qualities in others, they can tell when a person is thinking, processing and observing, and then give them the space to do so, which makes people feel much more comfortable, they allow time to really connect with people. They make quality friends, since introverts can feel their energy being drained by being around other people as opposed to extroverts, who gain energy from being with others. Introverts choose their friends wisely, they would rather have a few close, trusted friendships to invest their time and energy in, as opposed to a large network of acquaintances. Introverts are pretty picky about who they bring into their lives, it requires some energy, and if someone does come into their inner circle, that means a lot. This quality causes introverts to be loyal, attentive and committed friends.

They make loving romantic partners, introverts crave personal space to reflect and refuel, and they can sense when their partners need space too. Because we have this need for our own privacy, we give that to others as well, we won't be super clingy or high maintenance in relationships. And the same qualities that make introverts great listeners also make them great partners. At the end of a long day, they are there to listen and support their partner without feeling compelled to talk about themselves. They allow their partners to yell at them and let them release their emotions even if they are not at all involved in making them angry; introverts will apologize even if they haven't done anything wrong just because they cherish people more than their ego.

Introverts also like to get to know someone before sharing intimate details with a prospective partner, and it can make them appear more appealing in the early stages of relationships. There can be something attractive about the mystery factor of introverts, that can inspire curiosity and wanting to know the person better.

Introverts are thoughtful networkers, being in a large group where the goal is to meet, talk and make a good first impression can be overwhelming for many, especially for introverts. But they can use their natural strengths to create meaningful connections. Extroverts may approach networking events with the goal of talking to as many people as possible, but often, those quick conversations don't leave lasting impacts. But strength in networking is not necessarily in numbers. Introverts, should focus on learning about people they meet even if they only connect with a handful of people. Introverts try to make meaningful connections with a couple of people that they can follow up with in some way, after an event, they will send links to articles or speeches that made them think of the person that they spoke to. This type of active listening and follow-up can be a lot more beneficial than simply handing out hundreds of business cards, I believe.

Introverts can make the best leaders, when they channel their natural strengths. They don't feel the need to step into the spotlight and take all of the credit for group successes; rather, they are likely to highlight the strengths of their teams. An extroverted leader may be noticeable, but you may see the leader before you see the team. And employees who feel recognized tend to be more motivated. And since introverts process information more slowly and thoughtfully than their extroverted counterparts, introverted leaders tend to learn more about their subordinates. They have focused conversations with their team members in order to learn their skills, passions and strengths. Once they gather all of this information, they can use what they've learned to help each team member be more efficient and happier at work. When I started with these dating websites, I met a girl who was a nice match, it was because of her that I got encouraged to write. It was the first time when I talked to someone continuously over the phone for hours, I liked talking to her but soon we realized we were not made for each other, we are still in touch and we are really good friends now. Once in a while we send messages to see what are happening with other person's life and how is life treating them.

I would be the one who would solve questions and riddles in the class first but won't say a single word until asked about it. The best way to treat an introvert is to make them feel that you want an inclusive society where they get a sense of belonging and they see themselves as a part of the flock. Never try to push them away from their group, they may survive being a loner but that will become their habit and they will start hating social interactions slowly and slowly.

It's a myth th at everyone is born with the character that they carry, the reality is that we acquire it from the people around us, our family, friends and especially our parents, a child's mind and character is like water, put it in a jug and it will become a jug; put it in a bottle, it will become a bottle ; put it in a bowl it will become a bowl.

The worst you can treat a child is with anger and the sense of inferiority; if a child will not enjoy their parents' company there are higher chances that they will become introverts. If you keep on beating, scolding and controlling them the child will definitely be a timid person and they may turn out to be an introvert, when they grow up. If you make your kids feel inferior in front of others and expect too much from them to a level where they feel pressurised, this is definitely going to impact how they will perceive the world and their way of dealing with the society will be impacted thus another introvert will be born.

Chapter 23: Introverts And Relationships

When you are viewed as arrogant or withdrawn, as many introverts are, it can be a bit difficult to have healthy interpersonal relationships. Introverts absolutely love to curl up with a great book. They love to write, practice yoga, and engage in other solo activities, so it can be hard to bond with other people. They can also be shy and nervous with new people, which also makes it difficult to form relationships. If you find it hard to break out of your introvert shell, then this chapter is going to help you tremendously. From boundaries, tips and more, you can use this chapter to help form new relationships and repair or strengthen old ones.

Breaking Out of the Introvert Shell

This section will give you tips on how to break your shell. Some of the tips may sound difficult or nearly impossible, but it will be very beneficial for you to follow them.

●Do things that you are afraid of: You need to look for new ways to challenge yourself by meeting people and taking on different projects that you may have fear of. Typically, the project will turn into a surprising success. Normally when an introvert challenges their fear of meeting new people, they will walk away making a new friend.

●Volunteer on projects: Volunteering opens the door to making new friends by offering a service, which opens the door to bonding. Many friendships are made from this, no matter what type of personality you may have.

●Do not get distracted by your electronic devices: Today's devices are great, however, they can distract you from life happing all around you. Being consumed by the latest Internet trends of hot videos on YouTube will ultimately take your attention from those around you and you will miss opportunities to make friends that could be your partner in crime. Leave your device at home when you happen to be in social situations, or at least make a conscious effort to turn it off completely and be aware of your surroundings for a time. Do not allow yourself to use the protective bubble of technology to separate yourself from your environment.

•Connect with a friend over coffee, a picnic in the park, or just a quick lunch: It is very important to stay connected to those who are already in your life. Being an introvert, it is hard to force yourself to go out, however, it is very simple to have a quick bite or even a couple cups of coffee and small talk. The hardest thing will be to make the plans and actually follow through with them, but you will find that once you get there you actually enjoy yourself and feel rejuvenated.

•Ask questions about the person you are trying to get to know: Asking questions about a person's history, goals, and opinions is a great way to get to know them. It is an excellent strategy to get rid of the nervous energy that may accompany introversion, as it takes the focus off of yourself. They will feel like you really want to know them, and it will forge a bond and establish rapport. Do not worry about running out of questions; there are always questions to ask of the answer they gave to the first question. It will come naturally if you just keep going and remain genuine.

Three Crucial Boundaries Tips for Introverts

One of the largest challenges that an introvert will face is learning how to have a healthy relationship with boundaries. There are many people who have grown up thinking that their need for solitude is wrong. For many introverts, asking for some space will stir up feeling of unworthiness or guilt. This makes it very difficult for introverts to set boundaries that are healthy in their relationships.

They may even become so desperate to please their loved ones that they set aside their own needs. Many introverts will keep their own desires hidden as if it was unethical to want time alone.

The other tendency of an introvert is to be independent. Introverts tend not to depend on people, and when they do, it is not without much consideration. Boundaries should be healthy and unshakable when it comes to any acquaintances, and even many friends. So, how does an introvert set healthy boundaries in relationships? Here are three major tips that can be utilized for healthy boundaries.

●Do it right off the bat: A big mistake that an introvert makes often is waiting too long to speak about boundaries. This is typically due to shame. The introvert feels guilty about asking for time alone, so they put it off. When the introvert finally expresses what they need, the other person will feel confused and may even feel hurt. They do not understand why it is alright for them to call out of the blue one day, but now it causes problems. They are not able to understand why the introvert all of sudden needs their space, when just a few weeks ago they spent almost every waking moment together. Prevent confusion by setting the boundaries early in the relationship.

●Spread your attention around to a circle and not just one friend or loved one: If you find that one person who does not exhaust you while they are around, then you probably spend a lot of focus, attention, and time on them. This is not healthy for either of you. It is important to spread your attention around to a circle of friends rather than just one. There are other people in your life and you should share your attention.

●Give permission to yourself: Some introverts are stuck in the childhood mindset of needing permission. Introverts expect others to give permission and tell them what behavior is acceptable. Here are a few examples of what you should give yourself permission for:

○Spend just one day of the week or weekend by yourself without feeling any guilt.

○Politely say no to group and couple activities that you do not enjoy.

○Go on a small trip once a year without anyone else.

Being an introvert can be hard at times; however, it can be great too. If you follow these tips it will make your life a little crazy at first, but you will get used to them and you will be better for it without sacrificing your personality.

Introverts and Dating/Marriage

Introverts can have a hard time when it comes to dating due to their personality. Here are some tips to help you date in a healthy manner.

●Fess up to your personality: Do not pretend that you are a social butterfly. There is nothing horrible about being an introvert. Just politely explain to your date that you are a person who seeks friendship at first or needs some time to fall in love. You may scare a few away, but you do not want them anyways because they do not understand your personality and would not have a healthy and happy relationship. You will instead, attract those who will appreciate your personality.

●Meet in places that are comfortable to you: If you do not like bars, then do not go to them; it is that simple. You want to make sure that you are in a comfortable place to make you feel at ease. Often times introverts are pleasers too and they do what they may think the other person wants, even if they suffer for it. Find a good place that you feel comfortable in, possibly a coffee shop. You may even like the park.

●Avoid the smooth talkers: When you are in a relationship it is important that you are heard. If you are on a date and it seems as if you cannot talk or get a word in, then you should not be on that date. This person is not a right match for you.

•Look for small connections: At times introverts get flooded by first impressions and can ignore things that they should look out for. Ask yourself if you like being there. Do you feel crowded, nervous, or overwhelmed? Ensure that you actually like being with this person and that you genuinely have things in common.

•Beware of the takers: It has already been stated that introverts are givers. They listen, pay attention, and they want to be there for their loved ones and those around them. Ensure that you get to be on the end that receives too. If you must repeatedly ask for romantic gestures, to be included or for some consideration, this should be a sign that you do not need to be with that person.

Introvert - Extrovert Marriages

Even though there are differences, extroverts and introverts make great partners romantically. Maybe it is due to the fact that opposites attract, and what one partner does not have, the other does. They actually do balance each other out. Most extroverts express that introverts help them explore the more serious side of themselves. On the other hand, introverts are oftentimes grateful for their extrovert partners because it helps them make the atmosphere casual and lighthearted. They are also thankful that their extrovert does most of the talking in social situations, relieving a huge burden.

Conclusion

Thank you again for downloading this book!

You may have believed the disillusionment that being an introvert means you are lacking; you now know better. You are perfectly normal and highly capable. Introversion is not a fancy name for some mental condition as was once upon a time believed. The success rate for introverts can just speak for itself.

All the best in your quest.

Thank you and good luck!

www.ingramcontent.com/pod-product-compliance
Lightning Source LLC
Chambersburg PA
CBHW060322030426

42336CB00011B/1165